A NURSE ABROAD

A NURSE ABROAD

Adventures in Nursing from the Arctic
to the Outback

Anne Watts

WINDSOR
PARAGON

First published 2012
by Simon & Schuster
This Large Print edition published 2013
by AudioGO Ltd
by arrangement with
Simon & Schuster Ltd

Hardcover   ISBN: 978 1 4713 0988 5
Softcover   ISBN: 978 1 4713 0989 2

British Library Cataloguing in Publication Data available

Printed and bound in Great Britain by
MPG Books Group Limited

For all those who cherish our Earth

Contents

Author's Note and Acknowledgements vi

PART ONE: HOME AND AWAY

PART TWO: DOWN UNDER

PART THREE: CHANGING GEAR

PART FOUR: THE YEARS BETWEEN

Author's Note and Acknowledgements

Now retired from active nursing, I will nevertheless always have the dedicated nurse's responses to pain and suffering—especially when inflicted on those least able to help themselves: children, victims of conflict, the exploited and the dispossessed, everywhere in the world. Being a nurse is not only what you do, but it is who you are.

This drive to care for others fitted in comfortably with my desire to explore, and to learn about, our world—a desire that took shape in my childhood thanks to my sea-captain father's tales of adventure, and the thrilling windows on a wider universe that were opened for me by a gifted geography teacher at my school in Wales.

And so it was that nursing and travel have led me to an extraordinarily rich life, observing and working in many different cultures and circumstances all over the globe. I have made lifelong friends in a huge variety of places and had countless extraordinary adventures and experiences—not always pleasurable, but all of them enriching my insights into human behaviour and bringing the realisation that we really are a global village.

Such a life has given me many a tale to tell, and in 1999 I succumbed to the endless and persistent persuasions of friends, family and colleagues to share my story. This was a complete departure from everything I'd ever done or known, but I turned my thoughts to trying to write down the wonderful experience my life has been, and still is.

Following the death of my father on Easter Sunday, 1985, I was given a bulging, dog-eared package with my name written in his unmistakable scrawl on the front. Inside were all the long, newsy letters I had written to him from the time I had started travelling as a young nurse in the mid-1960s. In death he showed me what he could rarely speak of in life—his pride and vicarious enjoyment of the adventures of his 'Rambling Rose'. My youngest sister Joan told me this was his nickname for me. I had never known that.

What a wonderfully rich resource to have, my own words from real time. I read all my letters several times over, then set to work.

It was a long, long haul, written alongside some private nursing positions to keep body and soul together, but by 2010, to my utter amazement, my efforts resulted in the publication of *Always the Children*—and a contract to write a second book, filling in the necessary gaps of the first.

Here is that book.

*   *   *

Once again, as with *Always the Children*, I owe a debt of gratitude to many people who made this second volume possible.

Carlo Misouri for polishing my rusty Italian, Nikki Ould for demystifying the Glaswegian dialect of the 1960s. In Canada, Sally Wright, fearless and frontier-busting, and her partner Jean Paul Pinard, who both constantly promote sustainable lifestyle choices away from a dependency on fossil fuels, gave me hospitality and help, and showed me the possibilities for a different way of being.

I would like to record my appreciation and admiration to Cree warrior-woman and poet Connie, who writes so eloquently of the disdain shown to so many, and who so generously shared her personal history with me; and to Susan Walton RN, a role model for nursing students everywhere, a huge thank you for her assistance.

At Alice Springs in Australia, the teaching faculty at Yirara College and the nursing staff at the general hospital were generous with their time and information; and the many townspeople I spoke with enabled me to piece together what had happened—for better and for worse—to the town and its people over the years since I lived and worked there.

Every writer should have a Robyn Karney in their life. Her literary skills, firm encouragement and kindly tolerance whenever I flagged ensured that this book was completed. Angela Herlihy, you got me across the elusive finishing line.

My agent, Isobel Dixon, is a constant source of encouragement, and I am very grateful to commissioning editor Kerri Sharp at Simon & Schuster for her faith in me.

Anne Watts, Devon, 2011

Part One

HOME AND AWAY

1

Working Girl

Like the heartbeat of a terrified bird, the thready pulse fluttered softly beneath my fingers. Eyes closed, the girl's long dark lashes contrasted with the worryingly pallid skin; the flush suffusing her cheeks, the shallow respirations and rigid abdomen spoke of the infection and fever invading her skinny body.

I silently willed the driver to step on it, but we both knew the eighteen-mile journey needed to be undertaken as steadily and evenly as was possible. Every jolt of the bone-rattling ambulance travelling along the country roads on that dark November night would cause the child further pain. The headlights scythed through the rainy darkness as I gently applied cooling compresses to her forehead and armpits. The ice in the bowl had melted soon after we left the school, the water sloshing from side to side with each bend in the road.

' 'Tis sair. 'Tis sair,' whispered the little girl, her heavy Glaswegian brogue for 'sore' barely audible.

'Nearly there, Shauna. Nearly there,' I said, as much to reassure myself as the ten-year-old child in my care.

Valuable time had been lost in the attempt to locate her feckless parents. Neither was sober when found, nor capable of understanding the predicament their child was in, much less able to sign the consent forms for the surgery that would

3

save her life. The surgical team were on stand-by to receive her, with the requisite papers ready to be signed by two surgeons.

I felt the tyres leave the bumpy country road as we moved smoothly onto the main road that would sweep us into the well-lit entrance of the emergency room at Edinburgh Royal Infirmary.

Within a few minutes the vehicle stopped and the kindly driver shouted, 'Hold on, lassie. Here we are.' The rear doors opened and to my enormous relief, two medical attendants immediately took over. Shauna, gripping tightly onto my sweaty hand, was gently placed on a trolley, her scrawny body barely discernible beneath the sheet and coarse red blanket used to swaddle her from the damp night air.

As we entered the busy department, Sister, resplendent in crisply starched navy blue uniform and pretty little muslin cap perched atop a tight, spinsterish perm, hurried to meet us. She smiled brightly at the child, took the file from me and we handed Shauna over to two doctors. The surgeon quickly examined the sick child and whisked her away to the operating room, hoping that the appendix had not yet ruptured.

Relief washed over me in waves.

Sister was kind, immediately seeing the anxiety fall away from my face.

'Lassie, you'll be needing a strong brew. And I'll have one with you. It has been a terrible night all together. That's my office over there. Sit down and get your breath.'

The department was busy on this wet night. Drunks, traffic accidents, broken bones, victims of domestic abuse—all the flotsam and jetsam of

4

humanity that ebbs and flows in any big city was there.

As I began to relax, I became aware that the atmosphere was different from the usual mood of an emergency department.

Walking into Sister's small, cluttered office, I was taken aback to see a young doctor seated at her desk. He was holding his head in his hands, shock and a few tears etched on his handsome face.

You don't see that every day.

I began to back out of the office in some embarrassment, almost careening into Sister carrying a tray of steaming mugs of strong tea.

'Here you are, Dr McVey. Drink up, dear. This will help the shock. I've put plenty of sugar in.'

I took my tea, and looked at her.

'Anne, you will not have heard the news. President Kennedy has been shot. The poor man is dead. I think we must pray for his wife at this time.'

And without the slightest hesitation, she began a heartfelt prayer, with Dr McVey, an American over for six months' study on an exchange programme, and me joining in.

It was 9 p.m. on 22 November 1963 in Edinburgh, so it would have been 3 p.m. at the Parkland Memorial Hospital in Dallas, Texas.

My thoughts turned to the dismay of the American people in general, and the hospital personnel at Parkland in particular. I felt utterly helpless as I looked into the stricken face of this young doctor. In this famous Scottish teaching hospital people stood around in confused silence, trying to take in the news of the assassination, just

5

as they would be across the Atlantic Ocean.

The child fared better than the president. Her ready to rupture appendix was removed and she made a successful recovery.

There was never a word from her parents.

*　　*　　*

Towards the end of 1963, I emerged from five years of nurse/midwife study, blinking into the dazzling sunlight of life unfolding ahead of me.

From earning the measly sum of £9.10s (£9.50) a month, I was about to earn £13 per fortnight. The big time! And the world really opened up for me. Fully qualified nurses were in great demand in those days throughout North America, South Africa, Australia and New Zealand. Many girls in my class were engaged, soon married, became pregnant and quickly moved away from all they had been studying. What happened to their nursing dreams?

Even I had a fiancé. Well, it was expected of you, wasn't it? The sparkly ring, fathers relieved, mothers busily planning the wedding down to the finest detail—the dress, the church, the house, exactly where the engagement presents would be placed. Everything was happening so fast, with no apparent controls. It was like being on a runaway train and I watched in a state of temporary paralysis as others planned the rest of my life.

The day I overheard my stepmother saying, 'Well, *they're* buying them the bedroom suite, so we will have to buy the dining room suite,' was when I wised up.

Barefoot, pregnant, chained to the kitchen sink

and forever polishing matching furniture was not for me.

The end was messy. My one regret was that I hurt a decent young man, but better then than later. Jeff was lots of fun. A buttoned-up salesman of Cadbury's chocolates during the week, at weekends he was a bass player in a smoky jazz club. Highly unsuitable, according to my father, which was half the attraction, of course. His parents were sweet people who lived in a terraced house with terrible wallpaper, and who wanted nothing more in life than for their son to settle down nearby with a nice girl and raise lots of children. Scary stuff.

*　　　*　　　*

I decided, along with two nursing classmates, Ruth and Barbara, to experience nursing in Canada. This decision was rather helped along by my father, who would absolutely not hear of me going anywhere else. We had family in Saskatchewan and British Columbia who would keep an eye on me.

It appeared that the most manageable method of putting this plan into action was to go through the emigration process and travel by sea. The fare from Liverpool to Montreal was a whole £60. My God, a fortune! Our parents gave their blessings, but naturally we would have to fund ourselves. I think they thought we would fall at the first fence and turn our energies to something closer to home, but we three girls resolved that 1963–4 would be dedicated to raising the fare, and so the quest for paid employment commenced.

7

My first position was with the BNA agency. The British Nursing Association catered for 'nice girls' looking for a suitable position. While visiting friends in Edinburgh, I landed a temporary position at a residential school for disadvantaged children in Scotland. Their permanent nurse had fractured her femur when playing in a staff-versus-pupils soccer match. I liked the sound of that—the soccer match, that is, not the fractured femur.

The school was based in the pretty village of East Linton, about twenty miles east of Edinburgh. Coming from North Wales, I felt quite at home in the magnificent scenery.

The children, who came to the school from the Gorbals area of Glasgow, arrived in groups of forty or so and stayed for three weeks at a time. It was the first time I had met British children who had never climbed a tree; who knew only grim backstreets, where violence and deprivation thrived. Many were bed-wetters and stutterers, seemingly unused to encouraging words, wholesome food or cheerful optimism. Fights were common and I was constantly patching up the results of aggressive behaviour, ranging from a drumstick thrust into an eye to vicious fist fights. I could have used an interpreter because the thick Glaswegian accent was frequently incomprehensible —and what little I could understand was often the foulest language I had ever heard.

Lessons focused on sport—and appreciation of the natural beauty surrounding the alpine-style chalet dormitories that housed the kids, cared for by adults who took time to listen to their stuttering, surly words. There was sadness when each group left. Though their 'holiday' was short, most children benefited from these tranquil, ordered surroundings, but returning them to their troubled lives was distressing.

The school caretaker was a Polish veteran of the war. A man of few words, Josef had a good heart and could fix anything and everything. Broken desks, ruined mattresses, rotten goalposts and punctured footballs he took in his stride. He was also a master poacher.

The Scottish River Tyne (nothing to do with its much larger English namesake), which meandered beautifully between green fields along the south boundary of the school, positively heaved with salmon. At the end of each day, the staff really needed some relaxation, but teachers had as little money as nurses to spend on leisure pursuits, so we took to meeting with Josef at weekends in the trees bordering the river.

There, this wily fellow taught us the finer points of how to 'gaff' a plump, gleaming salmon. We all became quite proficient, and most weekends found us barbecuing the juicy steaks of these magnificent fish. With the innocent exuberance of youth and inexperience we revelled in our new skill until, one evening, the local gamekeeper caught six of us red-handed.

The whole thing had seemed like a jolly adventure right up to the moment we were summoned to appear in court. Josef was first in front of the Justice of the Peace and was given three months in jail, having been caught several times before. I remember almost fainting with terror. How was I going to tell my father that I was writing to him from prison? I considered stowing away on a ship and disappearing into the blue, never to be heard of again.

One of the teachers was a handsome Norwegian. His crafty plan was to speak only in his native tongue, pretending not to understand what he had been led into. I figured I would do the same, speak only Welsh, and plead ignorance. That would fox them!

Our pathetic defence never got off the blocks of course, and was dashed in an instant. The savvy JP wasted no time in ordering each of us to be fined sixteen guineas. My relief was enormous, though the sheer fright took ten years off my life.

It was only later I realized that my meagre savings for Canada had been blown to smithereens by our stupidity.

Despite my brush with the law, I loved my three-month tenure in Scotland and learned many new skills there (including how to poach salmon) that would come in useful in years to come.

2

Early Life

My childhood was definitely a game of two halves.

The early memories are a colourful jumble of cuddles and storytelling at my grandfather's knee, picking primroses with my mother, and falling out of venerable old oak trees with my giggling brothers and sisters.

At the age of nine, clouds began to slide across the sun, creating a gradual sense of foreboding, until tragedy struck. So began the second half, when, at the age of ten, I was catapulted into survival mode.

*   *   *

My father was a Merchant Navy officer, serving with the White Star Line, whose home port was Liverpool. Mother was a nurse at the Royal Infirmary, which is how I came to be born in that city in June 1940.

Evacuated from the blitzed city with many mothers and toddlers, we were sent to the safe haven of the mountains of Snowdonia, where my parents eventually settled, and where I was raised.

Father was a romantic figure to me, appearing at intervals in his uniform with its shiny buttons. He bore gifts from exotic lands and regaled us with stories of his travels.

Mother was a kind, compassionate woman with dark hair and an infectious laugh. She always seemed to be making corned beef sandwiches for the land girls and German prisoners of war who tended the farms in the area around our large country home.

When my father left the sea, one of the first things he did was place a large map of the world up on the breakfast room wall. Every day he would pick me up, stand me on a chair and the lesson began with a review of yesterday's lesson.

'Now, show me where the Gilbert and Ellice Islands are.'

My chubby little finger would meander over the chart, across the Pacific, coming to rest on the tiny islands he had circled faintly. He loved those islands. No doubt a woman was involved, but you don't know that at seven years of age, do you?

'Good girl. Now, where is Montevideo?'

Again my fingers would travel unerringly across to Uruguay.

And so my daily travels continued. I loved it, and grew up with a natural curiosity about the world I knew I would discover for myself one day.

It was decided by my father that the large house we lived in would make an ideal hotel, rather than a nursing home, which my mother would have preferred. As the business grew, my mother's health began to cause concern. There were visits to heart specialists in Liverpool, and episodes of collapsing, at church one Sunday, in the street another day.

Father employed a cook/housekeeper called Mrs Rigby. She was an excellent chef, and enhanced the reputation of the hotel as it continued to grow. But she had a terrible temper and we soon learned to keep clear of the kitchen.

One day, my five-year-old sister Susan and I were taken off to Liverpool by family friends for what we thought was a holiday. Instead, confused and frightened, we were left in a care home. In the late 1940s, in post-war Britain, there was a terrible emotional ignorance, and we were told nothing.

One day Miss Beard, the headmistress, summoned me to her office and told me my mother had 'gone to live with Jesus'.

That was it.

A short time later, my father arrived to take us home. At his side was the frosty-faced cook. Again, it was Miss Beard who informed us that 'this is your new mummy'. And we left for home. Two little girls in a state of shock.

Mother was never, ever mentioned again. A son was born to the cook five months later.

So began the second half of my childhood.

It was not until one summer's day in 1955, five years after my mother's disappearance, that I was told by a chambermaid that my mother had hanged herself and was buried in an unconsecrated grave by the village church.

I vowed that day never to let anything cause me such pain ever again.

* * *

I realise now that I have always been an amalgam of my parents—a big-hearted nurse who loves travelling and experiencing all the different cultures that make up our fascinating world. And thank God I also inherited my father's keen sense of humour. I have needed it in spades!

There was a serious stand-off between father and daughter when it was time for me to take up nurse training. He would not sign the consent papers, declaring, 'No daughter of mine will spend the rest of her life wiping other people's arses. I will not have it. That is my final word.'

We'd see about that.

My training at Manchester Royal Infirmary's School of Nursing began in 1958. After five wonderful, fascinating years, I graduated and was presented with my bronze Manchester Royal Infirmary 'penny', which I have worn with pride throughout my nursing career.

I was ready. Was the world ready for me?

3

Bella Italia

Leafing through *The Lady* magazine in early 1964, between the constant drudgery of the hotel chores to be got through at home, I applied for a position as nanny to a family in Italy. I reckoned I could save most of the generous salary being offered and, at the same time, learn some of the language.

It was only when I was at Heathrow, about to embark on the flight to Venice, that I called my father. I did not flinch at my thoughtless behaviour, as in those days we often clashed badly. He blew a fuse, grimly predicting that I would end up being 'sold as a white slave' and did I not know what Italians were like? Trying to reassure him, I replied that no, I didn't, but would find out and let him know, and anyway, what was a white slave? Maybe this was my way of punishing him for the way my mother's death was treated. He told me nothing, so why should I tell him of my plans?

That trip was the first time I ever flew. It was a strange sensation, the plane rising steeply, forcing my head back onto the headrest as the engines vibrated much more noisily than they do today. For a moment I wasn't at all sure where my stomach might end up as I gripped the arms of my seat. This was an exciting new dimension to living. The plane banked sharply to the left, and I looked down at the green rolling hills of southern England as we hurtled through clouds towards the Mediterranean.

14

I was met by Madame Russo, the beautiful Danish woman who was the mother of the little girl I would be caring for. Immediately insisting I call her Ria, she took me on a white-knuckle ride through sixty miles of rolling, fertile countryside. Passing manicured vineyards, silvery olive groves and fields studded with the cypress and conical evergreen trees so typical of the area, we began the gentle climb into the pre-alpine Euganean Hills. I was enchanted by the scenery. The light seemed softer, different from wintery Britain with its grey skies and drizzly rain. This was wintery Italy but the sky was pale blue, with fluffy white clouds. The hillsides were a mosaic of varying shades of green. Here and there farm buildings or a cluster of homes came into view, looking for all the world like a painting, so bright were their red-tiled roofs, so creamy their walls. As we bypassed Padua and purred through the small, picturesque town of Monselice, we approached our destination, the walled, medieval village of Arquà Petrarca.

My natural British reserve took a battering on that journey. At regular intervals, Ria would roll down the window and hurl abuse, loudly and liberally, at other drivers, who hurled it right back. I found myself sliding down in my seat, trying hard to look like I was anywhere but there. So it was that my first Italian phrases were *cretino di Venezia* and *porca miseria* ('cretin from Venice' and 'miserable swine').

It took months for me to relax enough to realise

that this was just a part of the scene and everyone did it. Italian passion reverberates through everything that's done—and said. Great dramatic gestures with voices raised were not altercations, as I thought, but simply ordinary conversations. This was so different from my own culture, but I grew quite accustomed to it in time and learned to enjoy the whole experience.

The Russo family home was a rambling, red-roofed villa of honey-hued stone. It was perched on a hillside overlooking the village where the poet Francesco Petrarca—better known to us and to Shakespeare as Petrarch—had lived the final part of his life and was buried in 1374.

On arrival, I was shown to my large, airy room where filmy net curtains moved slowly in the late afternoon breeze at the several large windows. When darkness fell, the faded green shutters were pulled to, keeping out the cool night air. I looked out over the rolling hills, captivated by the beauty of the surroundings.

After unpacking and freshening up, I went down to be introduced to the rest of the household staff: Flavia the cook, her husband Romano, who was the gardener and handyman, and Maria, the blushing teenage maid. Shyly welcoming, Romano greeted me in his halting English and told me they would teach me to speak Italian like an Italian. I immediately knew I would be happy there.

From the security of her mother's arms Sophia, my little charge, fourteen months old, gave me the once-over with that wide-eyed, steady gaze that toddlers have. I must have met with her approval because, with a sudden big grin that lit up the room, she stretched out her arms and came to me.

Just like that.

Later that evening, the man of the house arrived home from a business trip to Helsinki. Roberto was charming, effusive, full of life, and with a sharp sense of humour. I learned that he bought and sold mink and sable pelts, which involved him travelling regularly between Montreal, Helsinki and Leningrad (now St Petersburg).

So began a very happy year, a time when I learned much about all things Italian, and rather more than I wished to know about the Catholic faith.

*   *   *

Sophia was a delightful child. This did not seem like work at all, and the days passed quickly, filled with long walks, giggles and my efforts at Italian, which often reduced Flavia, Romano and Maria to helpless laughter. Something to do with my being unable to yell and gesticulate while speaking, I gathered.

'Signorina Anne. You are too Eeeengleesh! *Troppo calma. Troppo timida.* You must *feel* Italian —here, and here,' Romano would urge me, pointing to his heart and his belly.

As a foreign national, I had to report to the local police station in Monselice every Saturday morning to have my documents stamped and signed.

My day off was Sunday and that's when I explored my surroundings. I loved strolling in nearby Padua, the oldest city in northern Italy. Famed for its university and dominated by the beautiful Basilica of San Antonio, it was also a

17

place of pilgrimage, which added to the atmosphere for me.

I marvelled at the magnificence of Florence. It seems there was a sizeable colony of British students in the city, there to study art and language at the British Instituta based in the beautiful Piazza Santa Trinita. What a privilege to study amid such historical magnificence. Each twist and turn of the scenic little streets bustled with life and colour. Spanning the burbling waters of the Arno River was the medieval Ponte Vecchio. On either side of the bridge were tiny shops, originally small butchers' shops, which now sold artefacts, books and colourful handicrafts. I had never seen such sights or been surrounded by such a wealth of art and architecture, and Michelangelo's *David* surpassed every expectation.

I remember Clarks shoes were very fashionable, and handsome young men saved up for weeks for the classic footwear to go with their high-collared shirts and Lee jeans.

A new discovery for me was opera, which I first experienced and learned to appreciate in the glorious surroundings of the Roman Coliseum in Verona. Taken there one evening by Roberto and Ria, I sat entranced by a production of *Carmen*, staged in the open air under an almost ridiculously starlit sky. Unforgettable, and unique to the amphitheatre in Verona, was the staging of 'The March of the Toreadors'. The music began softly at first, somewhere in the distance behind us, accompanying dozens of the townspeople who, having paraded through the streets in full costume, carried flaming torches that highlighted the passion in their faces as they marched into this ancient site as the music came to a spine-tingling crescendo.

The family took me to the important town of Loreto, where, like at Lourdes, thousands of pilgrims from all over the world converge to pray to the Virgin Mary for deliverance from their illnesses or disabilities. I was amazed and moved as I watched people of all ages in wheelchairs, on crutches, many terminally ill and accompanied by medical and nursing staff, filing past the shrine. Chanting prayers, they ran fingertips along the black marble plinth, where many thousands of fingertips of the faithful before them had created deep grooves over the years. Many pilgrims left notes of gratitude for the miracles attributed to the Virgin, together with dozens of crutches and callipers discarded as no longer needed. The depth of humility, faith and reverence I witnessed was new to me, and deeply touching.

*　　　*　　　*

My time in Italy was my first experience of living in a culture noticeably different from my own, although that difference was in the Italian temperament and approach to life, a difference in mood and style.

I became aware of how trendy 1960s London was perceived by others. In Italy, while fashion ranged from exquisite *haute couture* worn by the fashionable and wealthy of both sexes, to the tight flares and body-hugging shiny shirts sported by younger men, and the floral minis, white slacks and pastel-coloured tops popular with the girls, the clothes were nothing like the London fashions of

19

the time. Edgy, eccentric and eclectic: feather boas, fashion threads on a budget from Biba in Kensington, Audrey Hepburn-style A-line dresses with their geometric slashes of colour on white or black backgrounds. Psychedelic colours ruled for my generation, and trouser suits or miniskirts with white go-go boots would soon be practically a uniform all over London, but not so much in Italy.

Meanwhile, I learned to perch on the pillion of a trendy Vespa, my arms tightly encircling a dark-eyed, snake-hipped, handsome local Lothario. Nobody was wearing helmets then and the sense of freedom was exhilarating. I learned too how to drink delicious Italian red wines with water added, and I swooned to 'Amore Baciami' sung by the gorgeous Gianni Morandi. I bought that record and later drove everyone mad at home in Wales by playing it constantly.

Back in my Italian home, however, a few disturbing events opened my eyes further to cultural differences of the less appealing kind.

One day I found Flavia at the kitchen stove, stirring one of her delicious sauces but quite obviously red-eyed and distressed.

'*Cosa c'e, Flavia? Cosa c'e?*'

Turning towards me, spaghetti sauce dripping unheeded from the wooden spoon in her hand and onto the flagstoned kitchen floor, she broke down completely.

'*Anna, Anna. Mio figlio, mio figlio ... Gianni ...*'

Between her sobs, I thought I understood that four-year-old Gianni was not at home. Had he run away? Had he gone missing?

'*Calma. Calma, Flavia.*' Between her distress and my bad Italian, my imagination went into overdrive. I hugged her, placed the wooden spoon into the bubbling pot and sat her down at the table. I went to find Romano, who was studiously digging up potatoes in the kitchen garden.

With a deep sigh, he placed a reassuring hand on my arm as he explained that they had given Gianni—their apple-cheeked youngest son—to the monks at the *seminario* above the village. This apparently was customary and a source of pride to families. I suppose the *seminario* could be described as a boarding school, where young boys were educated to a good standard.

In return, Romano and Flavia would receive, for the next twelve months, enough eggs, butter and milk to sustain their large family. The child would be raised at the *seminario*, his life dedicated to prayer and service until the age of sixteen, when he could choose to leave. Apparently few made that choice. It was considered an honour to give a son to the faith. (I had trained and worked alongside Irish nurses who spoke of how, in Catholic Ireland, it was fairly common for large families to have a son join the priesthood and, indeed, for a daughter to become a nun—or a nurse.)

It was a little while before I could quite take this in. If it was meant to reassure me, it did not and I then told Ria. She went instantly into a tirade about the goings-on in the village. She explained to me that, in the local community, the priest and the doctor ruled. All the ordinary working people were fearfully in awe of their religion, which was seemingly personified by these two men whom they obeyed without question.

Another time when I noticed Flavia looking worried and sad, she told me one of her other

21

seven young children was sick and she could not afford the medicine. A consultation with the doctor cost money, as did medicine or any other treatment that was prescribed, and only the doctor administered the medication. Flavia was saving up to buy syringes, needles and vials of antibiotics from the *farmacia*; she would then have to pay for each of seven daily visits to the doctor for the administering of the medication. Coming from a country with a national health service, where this simply could no longer happen, and being a trained nurse to boot, I was absolutely horrified.

I visited young Paolo, the child in question, and found him feverish with a nasty chest infection. I went out and bought the syringes and the drugs myself and told Flavia that I would give the boy his daily injection. Far from being relieved, she was terrified, and said the doctor would ask the priest to put a curse on me!

I reported all this to Ria. Generous, supportive and fiercely protective of her staff, whom she regarded as part of the family, she snorted with contempt for the doctor and immediately covered the costs involved. Reassuring me that I had nothing to worry about, she told me to go ahead with Paolo's treatment.

So I did.

Nothing more was said, and Paolo very quickly recovered.

*　　　　*　　　　*

Around noon one June day the skies suddenly and swiftly darkened, and the air seemed heavy with an almost ominous silence. The gloom was pierced by flashes of forked lightning and the silence broken by rolling thunderclaps. For some twenty minutes, a dramatic hailstorm hammered down on the countryside, battering cars, houses and a few unfortunate people. As soon as the spectacular downpour ended, summer skies and blazing sun quickly returned.

About an hour later, we heard chanting coming from the hillside below the house. Maria and Flavia immediately took fright and hid behind the door of the larder. Bewildered by this, I went out to see what was going on and there, wending their way slowly up the hill, was a procession of choirboys, led by the priest, who was sheltered under a large, heavily embroidered canopy, held over him by four teenage bearers, while other younger boys carried incense burners. All wore full high Catholic Church raiment.

The chanting was quite beautiful, but what was this all about? I called Ria, who looked out of the window and then, with her characteristic snort of rage, marched outside to await the priest, arms crossed and stance fierce. I could hear Maria praying loudly in the larder. The procession continued slowly around the property and came to a halt in front of Ria. I stood behind her, holding Sophia and feeling as though we were in the stand-off scene in *Gunfight at the O.K. Corral*, as she and the priest squared up for the fray.

The singing of the choirboys grew ragged and stuttered to a stop as the two antagonists, Ria and Father Domenico, apparently spewed out a stream of Italian vitriol at each other. I had to remind myself that in this part of the world passions ran high and shouting did not necessarily mean anger.

23

'*Perche tu sei venuto qui?*' asked Ria. (Why are you here?)

'*Sono venuto qui per dare Benedizione.*' (I am here to perform a Benediction.)

'*Al Prete. Non credo in quello che dici!*' (I do not believe you.)

Within a few minutes the priest turned and led his procession to retrace their steps towards the village below.

Ria explained to me that the priest said the *grandine*, or tempest, had stripped the vines, ruining the valuable crops in the area. The blame lay directly with the sins of all women of child-bearing age, and he had been sent by God to 'cleanse' all such women in the locality.

It took Ria a few days to calm down, Maria and Flavia a few hours to stop shaking, and me a while to get my head around the obvious damage such beliefs can wreak upon people who cling so tightly and hopefully to their religious faith.

But I also came to realise that what we were witnessing was a clash of cultures, of beliefs and of time. Ria was from Denmark, where Scandinavians generally were more open-minded and free to express themselves. In many parts of Europe, including my own country, such changes did not begin until the mid-'60s and erupted in 1968 with the student riots in Paris, London and elsewhere with anti-establishment and anti-Vietnam War passions. Students began questioning and challenging authority. In Italy the Catholic Church began to be challenged over divorce and abortion.

On this sunny morning in June 1964, I watched as a blonde Danish woman railed against a priest

24

whose job at that time dictated that he maintain the strict rules dictated by the papacy in Rome. This was a clash like no other I had seen.

Maybe both were right. They were just coming at each other from different moments in time.

*　　*　　*

All too soon my year as a nanny came to an end. I had to press on, and by now I had really begun to miss nursing. Roberto took me to his vast, temperature-controlled warehouses on the outskirts of Venice and showed me what seemed like acres of mink and sable pelts graded by colour, size and quality.

'Anna ... I want you to choose a pair of mink for yourself. They will make a beautiful hat or gloves, or a trim for a special dress, maybe. I want you to choose.'

I was completely nonplussed, and quite horrified at the scale of death draped on special hangers in this place. In the end, Roberto chose for me—a beautiful pale-blonde pair of mink, their little ears and noses, and the spaces where their eyes had once been, turned blindly towards me. He wrapped them reverently in tissue, and placed them in a box.

I headed for home, my precious fare to Canada—and enough to cover living expenses for a while—safely tucked away in my new bank account.

I never wore the mink, and never attempted even to have anything made up from them, but kept them stored in a suitcase for years. Occasionally I would take them out and stroke the beautiful fur gently, remembering my Italian interlude, and the family whose lives I had been privileged to share.

Some eight years later, while travelling around Europe with a group of friends, I paid a visit to the Russo family. There had been great changes.

Roberto had given away his business in fur and had become a recluse. He was now a practising Buddhist and a vegan, who spent his money rescuing animals from vivisectionists. Tearfully, he took me into the back garden, now transformed into an animal sanctuary. He introduced me to dogs, donkeys, rabbits, cats, pigs and monkeys, with all manner of signs of experimentation carried out on them. This man who had been president of the local shooting club, had hunted with the best of them, enjoyed his meat, and dealt in animal pelts, had been through a cataclysmic turnaround—some sort of breakdown, which had led to a crisis of conscience about his former life of killing animals for financial gain.

He seemed vulnerable, a shadow of his former self, yet I sensed an inner calm in him, acceptance that this was what he now wanted from life. Ria was still her elegant self, but was quieter, older, and looked tired. Sophia, now a schoolgirl, was away visiting her grandparents in Venice. Romano was still tending the grounds, but only two days a week; Flavia, sadly, had died of cancer just the year before. Time had moved on for all of us.

4

A Hero Laid to Rest

I arrived home just in time for Christmas 1964, happy to be with my sister Joan again after so long. As always, she was working all hours in the family hotel for little thanks, my stepmother's tongue was as sharp as ever, and Father was running around dementedly as the hotel buzzed with guests.

I was quickly put to work too, and found myself lapsing into dramatic, Italian-inspired gesticulations and phrases as I waited on tables, washed dishes, made beds and cleaned lounges. But, best of all, I served wines with a continental flourish that left local staff open-mouthed with what I liked to think was admiration but was probably nothing of the sort.

Spaghetti, garlic and pizza withdrawal symptoms were kicking in, but playing my Gianni Morandi love ballads eased the suffering, and sharing my stories and giggling with Joan helped the days go by for both of us.

The all-important date in my calendar was 4 February 1965, when Barbara, Ruth and I had to attend interviews at Canada House in London, where we would finally be approved or not—for eligibility to immigrate to Canada. By now we were reasonably solvent, a point in our favour.

*   *   *

On 15 January 1965, a radio news bulletin

27

reported that Sir Winston Churchill had suffered a debilitating stroke. It seemed to me that my father, and all British men and women of his generation, held their collective breath until, at 8.35 a.m. on 24 January, a very cold winter's morning, a statement announcing his death was read out to the huddle of reporters gathered outside the Hyde Park Gate home of the great and inspirational wartime leader.

My father was visibly upset and immediately walked out of the house and across the lawn to adjust the fluttering Union Jack and Red Ensign on his beloved flagpole, which he'd erected on his own return from serving in the Merchant Navy during World War Two. Now he lowered his flags to half-mast and, stepping back, stood to attention for a few moments, then murmured a prayer before walking slowly back to the house. Several men and women in the village came to the hotel, to see 'the Captain', as Daddy was affectionately known, as if gathering together gave them some comfort.

The date of the funeral was announced, to be preceded by three days of lying in state in Westminster Hall. Winston Churchill would be the only commoner to be given a state funeral in the twentieth century.

To my parents' generation, Churchill both symbolised and embodied man's will to resist tyranny, and his dynamic leadership had sustained the country in her hours of truly darkest need. My father, longing to go to the lying-in-state, was so torn between wanting to pay his respects to one of his heroes, and knowing that the hotel was very busy and could not simply be left.

As the eldest of several children, and aware of the depth of my father's feelings in such matters, I volunteered to go down to London as his representative. The relief on his face told me I had made the right decision, but I was doing it for him and certainly had no idea of what an extraordinary and rewarding experience it would prove to be for me.

I travelled to London on a cold, draughty overnight coach, and arrived at Victoria coach station to find it a moving scene of a city in sorrow. Trains, buses and businesses, from small corner shops to huge department stores, had draped the sides of their windows in black; men wore black armbands, and many women were dressed in black. The very air carried a tangible sense of loss, mingled with reverence.

A police officer directed me to Millbank, where I joined the long lines of people waiting to pay their respects. For a good four hours we quietly moved forward—across Lambeth Bridge, past St Thomas' Hospital, across Westminster Bridge—heading towards Westminster Hall. The weather, though thankfully dry, was grey and bitterly cold.

I stood in line alongside a young man who was pushing his grandfather along in a wheelchair. The still distinguished-looking gentleman was much advanced in years, as was evident from his wispy white hair and his hunched and shrunken body. He was well wrapped up in a heavy tweed overcoat and a woollen scarf, but his baggy gloves were unable to disguise the cruel twisting of arthritic fingers. A lopsided row of military medals was pinned across his chest.

Naturally, we fell into conversation. The old

29

man, who introduced himself as Harry McMaster, was so proud of his grandson, Andrew, who was studying medicine at the nearby St Thomas's Hospital, and Andrew was equally proud of his war veteran grandfather. Andrew told me that, ironically, his own father, an army officer, had been killed in France during the war. As we chatted, I explained I was there to pay respects on behalf of my father, a retired Merchant Navy master mariner too busy, and maybe too upset, to attend himself. With obvious emotion, the old man acknowledged the vital role played in the war by the Merchant Navy.

All around us, so smart in their school uniforms, wound crocodiles of children chaperoned by primly fussing schoolteachers; also making their way slowly along were the Boy Scouts, Girl Guides and the Sea Scouts; servicemen and women, young and old, were there in their hundreds, as were ordinary people of all ages drawn from every background, rich and poor alike. Shivering together in the cold, they were united in their single-minded determination to pay their respects to Winston Churchill.

Eventually, I had to ask my new friends to save my place in line while I went off in search of something warm to cover my head and ears, now aching in the cold wind. I found a vendor doing a brisk business selling hideous synthetic fur hoods that buttoned up under the chin. Counting out my precious pennies, I bought one, plus three scalding-hot paper cups of Bovril, and took them back to share with grandson and grandfather. That crummy-looking hood saved me from ending up with galloping earache.

30

Later, a gypsy flower-seller moved up and down the long lines, trying to interest people in her little sprigs of 'lucky white heather, dearie', or small bunches of purple violets. I had just enough money left to buy two bunches of the delicately shy violets—my father's favourite flower. I would leave them as close to Sir Winston's coffin as I could, I thought—just a small token that seemed somehow fitting.

Slowly but steadily the lines of mourners advanced forward to Westminster Hall. Immediately before it was our turn to enter, a policewoman stepped forward. She looked pointedly at my posy of violets and said, in a kindly but firm tone, 'You can't take those in with you.' I explained I had travelled down all the way from North Wales on behalf of my father who was deeply upset, and that he would love these flowers to be left as a symbol of his respect. She took them from me, examined them carefully, consulted with a senior officer and then returned them to me with a smile and a nod.

We passed into the magnificent Hall, originally built in 1097. Predating the present Houses of Parliament, this, the oldest parliamentary building, had evolved over a period of 900 years. Extraordinarily, given in whose honour we were there on that day, Westminster Hall had survived the Blitz unscathed. By now I was quite overcome with the sense of occasion and history. The breath seemed to catch in my throat, and the whole scene imprinted itself on my memory in the slowest of slow motion.

On a central plinth, up four steps and surrounded by a garnet-coloured carpet, sat the

31

catafalque. The bier was covered in black velvet edged with silver braid, upon which sat the coffin, draped in the Union Jack. Churchill's insignia as Knight of the Garter, including collar, star and garter, sat—proud yet, in my young romantic mind, forlorn—on a black velvet cushion on top of the coffin. A large, free-standing gold cross stood at the head of the coffin and four very large, creamy white candles glowed at each corner of the bier, casting soft light into the shadowy recesses of the Hall. And beside each corner—motionless like statues, heads bowed, and weapons reversed—an impeccably uniformed representative of the various armed forces stood guard.

Silently we filed past, two endless lines of people to either side of the bier. You could have heard a pin drop. How I wished my father was there to witness and share what I was seeing; my brother Hugh, by then in the RAF, would have been moved by this also.

As we drew abreast, Harry McMaster, the old soldier, very slowly and painfully hauled himself up from his wheelchair as far as his body would allow. While Andrew held the wheelchair steady, Harry placed his left hand under his right elbow as a support, then slowly lowered his head to meet his gnarled and crippled right hand in a final salute. The supreme effort required to make this gesture of respect was deeply touching. It was clear there was no way he was not going to salute the great Winston, no matter what it cost him in physical pain.

Fighting back tears, I stepped forward and placed the small bunch of violets on the top step, right next to the coffin. I knew the eagle eyes of those responsible for security were watching me closely, but nobody stopped me and I was very grateful for that.

As we left Westminster Hall, I knew, with a feeling of awe, that I had seen and been part of a piece of history.

*　　*　　*

Two days later, back in North Wales, the family gathered to watch Churchill's funeral on our crackly black-and-white television set. We wept with pride when the cranes at London docks dipped, in perfect unison, as the coffin was taken by launch to Waterloo, to continue its journey by train to Churchill's birthplace at Bladon, near Blenheim Palace, for burial. Many hundreds of people, including schoolchildren, lined the train's route to Oxfordshire.

And so Britain's great twentieth-century hero was laid to rest with moving and impressive ceremony that marked not only his passing, but the end of an era.

5

Bon Voyage

The fourth of February 1965 came around soon enough, and Ruth, Barbara and I nervously reported to Canada House, just off Trafalgar Square. As we sat filling out the forbidding forms, I was very worried as to how I should answer one particular question: 'Have you ever been convicted of a criminal offence?'

I thought back to the salmon-poaching incident, and blushed bright red remembering the consequences of it. Ruth said, 'For God's sake, they aren't going to worry about *that*,' but I couldn't so easily dismiss my only experience of stepping into a court of law and receiving the fright of my life. Clearly, despite spreading my wings in Italy for a year, I was still more naive than I would have liked to think, and struggled with how to answer for a good ten minutes!

If I wrote 'No' and was then found out, I'd be in trouble. If I said 'Yes', the great Canadian adventure would surely be strangled at birth. I decided the best thing to do was come clean and, before I could change my mind again, I made for the shortest queue. When it was my turn, I explained to the official behind the window that I was having trouble with this one question.

'Well, have you been convicted of a crime?' he asked, raising an eyebrow.

In a slightly shaky voice, with cheeks aflame, I told him of the Scottish episode, and the fine of sixteen guineas for poaching salmon.

He looked at me very intently for what seemed like an age before saying, 'You are just the sort of person we are looking for in Canada. Put no.' And then he smiled reassuringly.

I didn't smile back, but if he said it was OK, I supposed it must be . . .

And it was.

*　　　*　　　*

After two more months at home, the time came for a flurry of packing and tearful farewells to friends and neighbours and to my beloved sisters. My father and my brother Hugh, looking very handsome in his RAF uniform, came to see me off at Liverpool docks, along with Ruth and Barbara's families. Then, the goodbyes over, the last embraces exchanged, we boarded the coach that would take us to where the SS *Empress of England* was berthed. We moved to the rear of the bus and waved to the fast-disappearing knot of family members, tears prickling as the realisation of what we were doing began to sink in. Hugh told me recently that Father was so upset they went to a bar and had 'a couple of pink gins'.

I had no idea at the time.

So it was that on 6 April 1965, three excited young nurses boarded the *Empress of England* at Liverpool and set sail via Greenock for Montreal.

It was on this six-day voyage that I discovered I have very sound sea legs. The abstract of the log, which I still have, records conditions that varied between moderate breezes and rough seas. Each day, there were fewer people in the dining room

35

until by day five there was just a handful of us die-hards turning up for each meal. Both Ruth and Barbara were quickly restricted to our cabin, tended by the overworked ship's nurse and doctor who constantly made rounds to tend the many passengers left prostrate on their bunks.

Being on a large passenger liner was an education for me. I was amazed to find there was a cinema on board, and I happily watched a film every day. My favourite was *The Yellow Rolls-Royce* starring the beautiful Ingrid Bergman and the dishy Omar Sharif, and it was the film that made me a lifelong fan of the wacky Shirley MacLaine. They also showed *The Greatest Story Ever Told*, the first film I ever saw depicting Hollywood's idea of the life of Christ, which, strangely enough, brought tears to my eyes.

In the dining room, the first time I was presented with buckwheat cakes and sausages drizzled with maple syrup, I thought the chef must have gone off his head and confused breakfast with the lunch dessert. But no, this was my introduction to Canadian cuisine, which I quickly learned to enjoy.

In the evenings, the ever-dwindling group of passengers danced to the Jack Canter Orchestra in the Empress Room. Pretty soon there were only handsome young crew members left to dance with, which was fine by me.

As we entered the St Lawrence Seaway, icebergs could be seen on either side of the ship. I went up on deck and, trying not to think of the *Titanic*, watched the approaching land with a surge of excitement and anticipation as I wondered what this bright new world might hold for us.

6

Brave New World

Having been raised on the small island of Britain, my sense of land mass was naturally limited. Looking at a world map, one sees the spread of Russia, North America and Australia on the page, but that vastness means little unless you find yourself actually in one of these countries, travelling through its abundance of space.

After disembarking from the ship at Montreal, my own journey across the country began on board the sleek trans-Canada trains that would take me over a thousand miles to Saskatchewan, where my cousin and her family lived. Ruth and Barbara were continuing on to Vancouver, where I would join them later.

As the stately cities of Quebec and Ontario disappeared from view and the train began to carve its way through the prairies of Manitoba, the land seemed to fall away, leaving an expanse of clear sky that dominated the landscape. I gazed excitedly from the window of the speeding train and became aware after a while that, because of the stark flatness of the land, the horizon was much lower than any I had ever seen.

That night I bedded down in my comfortable berth and slept soundly, waking the next morning alert and eager to see where we were. Where we were was still on the prairie, stretching as far as the eye could see. All day the train thundered on, all night I slept well again, and all next morning still

37

the prairie landscape stretched endlessly in every direction. I was filled with a sense of awe at the sheer size of this land—yet we were still barely two-thirds into the journey to Vancouver, our ultimate destination.

As the train pulled into Saskatoon, I immediately recognised my cousin Betty, her small frame dwarfed by Charles, her handsome husband who towered over her.

Betty had tears in her eyes. I don't think she could quite grasp that a family member fresh out from England was standing in front of her. She still had that English rose look about her neat frame, despite the years of carving out a life for herself and her family in an environment that was so very different from her early life.

Hugs and kisses, and a flurry of loading bags into their truck, and we were off.

'Welcome to Saskatchewan. So, what do you think of the prairies?'

'I thought they'd never end!'

Charles was a man of few words, but he laughed, saying, 'Here you look out the window and can see for three weeks. You'll have to get used to it.'

As we bowled along the wide streets of Saskatoon I realised everything in this New World looked well planned and contrasted vividly with the crowded Old World I had just left. We soon left the suburbs behind and sped along a seemingly endless highway beneath a vast expanse of sky with little to break the distant horizon.

Betty was the daughter of my uncle, a Church of England minister, and had been raised with her three siblings in the genteel surroundings of a large vicarage in Formby, near Liverpool. She married Charles, the son of family friends, at the time a dashing officer in the Canadian Army, and in 1945 sailed for Canada and her new life, along with hundreds of other war brides.

Life would not have been easy in those early post-war years. The war brides had met with some resentment from the women of the prairies, many of whom had lost their men to the war or whose sons had survived only to return with foreign brides. These young women, coming from gentler climes, had to learn to endure the typical prairie life: harsh winters and stifling summers; cooking on wood-burning stoves in the small, wooden houses built by their men. No running water or electricity meant constant chores of hauling buckets of water from the ravine, chopping wood, trimming kerosene lamps and emptying the indoor toilet not yet plumbed in. Tubs of snow were melted on the stove for baths.

Charles farmed an area of 640 acres. The main crop was wheat, but rotation farming was practised to encourage the land to revive between wheat crops, so he also grew other crops such as barley or alfalfa from time to time. Some land was kept fallow for grazing cattle. The couple kept chickens and cows and had a vegetable garden. Sustenance hunting provided deer and ducks.

By the time of my visit, Betty and Charles had three healthy children: Heather, a vivacious eighteen-year-old, who must have had every red-blooded male for miles around yearning for one of her smiles; David, at fourteen, a tall, athletic lad who milked the cows and tended the horses; and lovable Robert, then only nine, who collected the

39

eggs and helped wherever he could. Farming is hard work and each had their chores, including Heather, who used to haul buckets of water from the ravine; in winter, this involved chopping a hole in the ice.

Thankfully, seven years before my visit, Charles had installed a generator and built a dam across the ravine, providing running water for bathing and washing clothes. Laundry was hung outside in all seasons and froze solid in winter, but when drying on a rack in the kitchen, their thawing created an exotically steamy and humid environment quite at odds with the climate! A battery-operated radio provided the all-important crop reports and news of world events and, occasionally, when the limited battery life allowed, the music that both Heather and Betty loved. Phones were on a party line and all calls went through Alice Spence, the central operator who certainly knew exactly what was going on in the community!

Everyone pitched in to help bring in the harvest, the fruits of which could be seen in the basement, which was crammed with rows of Betty's canned and bottled fruit, vegetables, marmalades, jams and chutneys. She was a wonderful cook and baker, quite renowned in the area for her bread, pies and cakes, and she taught me how to bake with sourdough, the simple and delicious recipe for bread, scones, cakes or pancakes, which had been used by settlers, pioneers and those living unostentatious lives for hundreds of years.

One day Betty took me to meet some friends of hers in Paynton, a small nearby village. I was fascinated by their story.

Winnie Taylor and Molly Webb were mother and daughter. On the day we rolled up for afternoon tea and a chat, they were both sitting in rocking chairs and were the most enormously obese people I had ever seen. Winnie was ninety years old, and her little wooden prairie home, a verandah running around three sides, was stuffed to the gunnels with furniture and bric-à-brac from another age. It should have smelled musty, but instead the delicious aroma of fresh baking and a faint scent of lavender wafted through the rooms.

It took a while for my eyes to adjust to the dim light, but when they had I saw a large, dark-wood, upright piano against one wall, with two brass candlestick holders sitting drunkenly on its front and surrounded by a decorative scrolled pattern in gilt. Blobs of candle grease, seemingly frozen in time, had long ago dripped slowly down from what was left of two candle stubs. Two well-used dark green armchairs and a brown settee were jammed into the small sitting room. Wherever there was a flat surface, no matter how small, pretty little glass or porcelain bowls were arranged on delicately crocheted mats. In a corner, grandly surveying the whole scene, stood a beautiful old grandfather clock loudly ticking time away.

Molly heaved herself out of her rocker, lumbered into the kitchen, and served us afternoon tea. It was all very traditional and 'proper': slices of Victoria sponge cake and deliciously fresh scones were served from a three-tier cake stand; the large teapot dribbled not a drop from the spout, and we drank from bone china teacups.

Winnie told me how her parents had brought all

41

these 'touches of home' with them when they sailed from England in the late 1800s, to make a better life in Canada.

'Of course, we lost a lotta stuff along the way,' Winnie said, throwing back her head and laughing uproariously. Just as well. They never could have squeezed another thing into that sitting room.

With many others, Winnie's family had crossed the country in covered wagons, suffering many privations. Reverend Lloyd, a Welsh minister with the group, officiated at funerals, marriages and baptisms along the way.

After more than three years of travel, shocked by the winters, and learning to live with the hot summers, in 1903 the people known as the Barr Colonists eventually settled and formed a community they named Lloydminster. This is where Molly was born.

I was enthralled by Winnie's tales and tried to imagine the piano, the grandfather clock, the delicate china and the intricate lamps being transported lovingly across this land in bumpy wagons. When we eventually left, I felt like a time traveller, stepping from one era to another, and back again.

It was clear that the people who came out to the prairie provinces, whether in the 1800s or in the mid-1940s, many from comfortable backgrounds, had very quickly to adapt and become self-sufficient. The more I learned of this life, the more I admired the determination those brave souls must have had.

7

Joie de Vivre

It was a late spring day in June 1965, my first full day in Vancouver, where I'd travelled to start my new nursing project, and I was trying to absorb my surroundings in this new, very different environment.

That day, as I walked around the city, I had the distinct sensation of looking through a giant magnifying glass. Main thoroughfares like Granville Street were so much wider than the roads I was familiar with in England; buildings were taller and everything looked squeaky clean. Instead of streets filled with grey buildings and grey people under a grey sky, Vancouver boasted orderly avenues of colourful, colonial-style timber houses, their lawns neatly tended. Flowering shrubs peeked over well-clipped hedges and I saw my first palm trees. Even the traffic seemed well controlled and I realised I had arrived in a new world, one very different from that of Europe with its crowded cities, world-weary inhabitants and the scars of its long history. Here, I felt exhilarated by the feeling that anything was possible.

Sunshine bounced off the sparkling Pacific waters of Burrard Inlet and English Bay, where sailboats bobbed in the wake of larger ships. Wholesome-looking people of all ages jogged through the magnificence of Stanley Park, one of the largest urban parks in North America. Back home, even after a few drinks, I never could have envisaged pensioners in shorts and T-shirts, with purple sweatbands encircling their damp foreheads, pounding the trails of their local park. In Britain, anyone over fifty seemed ancient, living out their twilight years in sedate austerity as we youngsters looked forward to finding ways to change the world and have some fun along the way.

Vancouver's natural sea port is dominated by the beauty of the North Shore mountains, and on a clear day you could see the snow-capped volcano of St Helens across the border with the USA in Washington State. And like its American neighbour, Canada had long attracted immigrant communities from both East and West. Chinatown, filled with mysterious sights, sounds and smells, covered a large area downtown and was a fascinating place to explore, while Robson Street was a magnet for the many Hungarians, Czechs and Poles who had converged here on the promise of a brighter future after the Soviet takeover of Eastern Europe. This colourful street was bursting with European delicatessens, as well as bistros and clubs that were a cultural home from home for the young East Europeans, cut off from their roots in their quest for freedom.

Of course, like any city, Vancouver had, and has, its ugly underbelly. In due course, I discovered Hastings Street and learned that not everything was as perfect as it seemed. This was the downtown area where the poor, the dispossessed, and those addicted to alcohol and drugs ended up. Every society has people who end up in the gutter, exhausted and unable any longer to cope with life but, for the time being, I was thrilled by everything

44

I saw and experienced, as one is when young and still relatively innocent.

Barbara and Ruth had found us an apartment in a high-rise block called Acapulco Towers on Twelfth Avenue. It seemed very glamorous to us, and we felt ready to take the world by storm. It was also a convenient ten-minute walk to Vancouver General Hospital, where I was about to begin twelve months as a Registered Nurse.

A seven-day orientation programme efficiently informed me of the hospital's rules and regulations and told me what was expected of me. I bought some smart white dresses, with white stockings and shoes to match, attached my Manchester Royal Infirmary hospital pin and was ready to go.

*   *   *

My first assignment was to the emergency room where, initially, I worked in the reception area as triage nurse. But before dealing with a new patient's medical history and emergency requirements, which is what triage nurses do, I had to accustom myself to the fact that the first essential check was into the patient's medical insurance cover. No cover, no treatment. No NHS. I had to get over my feeling of embarrassment at having to clarify a patient's financial arrangements.

The ER was a busy eighty-bed unit, divided into eight sections, with cases graded in order of urgency. It also had a cardiac unit, a resuscitation area and, tucked away in the back of this large department, six padded cells. Called the 'Quiet Rooms', these cells provided a safe environment

45

for alcoholics, drug addicts and disturbed psychiatric patients, protecting both them and the public until they were sent to a more appropriate clinical area for further treatment. After my initiation in the reception area, like all other personnel I began my rotation through the different clinical areas.

It was in the Quiet Rooms that I met my first North American Indians. They were brought in regularly (and often in a dreadful state) by the police or the ambulance services, and seemed generally to be regarded as the lowest specimens of humanity. In all honesty though, I was naive, enthusiastic and carefree, and it was quite a while before I learned something of the history of Canada's Indians and came to realise the full extent of the injustices they suffered.

The experience of working in the ER helped me to grow in both professional and personal confidence. I realised, as I observed and absorbed the methods used by both the doctors and the nursing staff, that—despite certain differences in practice from which I learned much—my training had been very solid and I could compete easily with those from other countries.

At each shift one nurse was assigned to administer all medications ordered, whether oral, intramuscular or intravenous. This was a new idea to me but I quickly realised how quick and efficient the system was. Rather unnervingly, however, a thick pad of printed 'Medication Error' slips sat at the side of the drug cupboard, and at the end of each shift several had been filled out. I asked what these were for exactly. An American nurse, impossibly glamorous and with long, scarlet fingernails that mesmerized me, explained, while chewing her gum, 'Honey, you fill out the details each time you screw up.' She wouldn't have lasted five minutes under Matron's eagle eyes at the Manchester Royal Infirmary!

Not only had I never witnessed a 'medication error' during my five years of nursing, but I had on only one occasion heard of an error being made. Nevertheless, I remained very much on my guard during my time in the ER and made sure I never had to fill out one of those forms—especially as I witnessed the results of several medication errors made by others.

As it so happened, by going to North America in the mid-1960s, my stay coincided with the height of the hippie movement: peace and goodwill to all men, flower power, free love. Many young Canadians were travelling across Canada, making for Haight-Ashbury in San Francisco, which was the hippie centre of America. A year or two later, ironically, many young Americans were fleeing to Canada to avoid the draft that would send them to Vietnam: a country and a war which would soon play a major role in my own life. I couldn't know that then, of course; I was more preoccupied with the consequences of the drug-taking that was also part of the hippie culture, and prevalent among the young.

Sadly, many of these idealistic but misguided young people were brought into the department suffering the ill effects of LSD, then the drug of choice. Often the LSD was reduced to a colourless liquid and little perforated squares of blotting paper were soaked in it. Once dry, they looked like stamps, but if your fingers came into contact with

47

them, the skin quickly absorbed the LSD. Handkerchiefs or tissues were also soaked in the liquid. After all, when searched by police on the street, what could be more innocuous than a tissue or handkerchief in your pocket? When you got to the party, the tissue was dropped into a bowl of water, and there you had it—a big party in a small bowl! So it was that I quickly learned always to wear protective gloves when looking through the pockets of semiconscious patients.

I was never tempted to experiment with drugs. Nursing those who came to grief was salutary warning enough. But, just like all young people down the ages, I could certainly see the world needed to change; equally I could see that the only thing that was changed by smoking dope or using hallucinogenic substances was yourself. It was self-defeating and a one-way road to grief.

Many of the casualties were brought in with fractured and badly lacerated fingers and hands, injuries sustained while in the grip of a hallucination. Such hallucinations frequently suggested bright light and windows where none existed. While 'tripping', the sufferer would scrabble madly at the bare walls, trying to get out of the nonexistent windows.

But sometimes there actually was a window. If the person crashed through it, ground level was OK. But sometimes the window was six floors up . . .

There were multiple injuries, and there were deaths.

The most difficult phone calls were those made to worried parents. On arriving at the hospital, they would have to be told how their child came by

48

such serious injuries or, worse, how their son or daughter had died. Often the kids were from affluent families. I was always struck by those well-heeled parents who clung to each other, saying, 'We don't understand. We always gave him/her everything he/she wanted.' They could never see that over-privileged indulgence might well have been part of the problem.

I knew then, and have certainly had the point reinforced over the intervening years, that happiness is not the elusive thing that so many seek throughout their lives. It is inside each and every one of us all the time. We need to recognise that we carry the key within us, and the life lesson is knowing how to turn it. Western society sets up its young to fail pretty early on with the message given that you will be judged in life by how much stuff you acquire; how big a house/car/career you have. Anything less and you will be judged a failure. No wonder drugs are often seen as an alternative escape from such a skewed view of what life needs to be about.

One of my favourite homilies is:

Life is not about waiting for the storm to pass. It is about learning to dance in the rain.

It is as true now as it was then.

49

8

Lessons in Life and Death

After six months in the emergency room, I was
assigned to the spinal-cord injuries intensive care
unit. This was probably the most demanding type
of nursing I have ever done, and it was here I
learned two powerful lessons in life.

* * *

Wayne Bull was twenty-one, with a generous head
of blond hair, a muscular physique and twinkly
blue eyes. In short, he was a hunk.

Wayne had been laughing happily in the bright
sunshine with his two friends, before diving into
the turquoise waters of a lake on Vancouver
Island. His head hit a submerged log, fracturing
the C2 vertebra—known as the 'hangman's
noose'—and, with a terrible immediacy, his neck
snapped. His limp body was quickly retrieved from
the water by his shocked friends, who made a
frantic call to the air rescue rapid-response
emergency service, who quickly arrived at the
scene by helicopter and flew him to VGH
(Vancouver General Hospital). Wayne was
immediately transferred to the ICU, where I was
assigned as his nurse.

He was paralysed, unable to feel any sensation
below his chin. He was also unable to breathe,
swallow, speak, urinate, or empty his bowels; in a
moment his life had changed irrevocably and

50

permanently. Above the chin, he was still Wayne, the security park ranger; lover of cold beers on a summer evening, rowdy games of pool with his mates, and the pick of the prettiest girls at the Saturday night dance in Nanaimo. But nothing would bow to his will again.

Oh yes, we did everything by the book. X-rays were taken (no scans in those days), intravenous drugs given to reduce the cerebral and spinal oedema; drugs to calm him, drugs to stabilise his shock. Everything of the best that medical science had to offer at that time was generously administered.

Wayne was the highest level surviving quadriplegic in 1966 Canada. Many venerable professors in the field of spinal injuries visited, prodded, and wrote papers that were well received at medical conferences, but Wayne knew, as I knew, that the effluent had hit the fan, that the life he had known was effectively over.

The four-bed research unit was a special place of study and care. We nurses worked closely as a team and were expected to put in twelve-hour shifts and stick with it until a comfortable rapport had been established with the shocked patient. Each patient was assigned three carers: a day nurse, a night nurse, and a third nurse who relieved the other two on their days or nights off. This arrangement enabled the patient to build up a close, trusting relationship with his carers, which is such an essential part of the healing process.

Most casualties who sustain spinal injuries are young. The damage usually happens as a result of accidents that occur during testing athletic activities such as diving, gymnastics, horsemanship and motor racing. There are seven vertebrae in the neck and all are vulnerable.

I nursed Wayne for eight straight weeks, sixty hours a week, two days off. I watched his shock, anger, fury, denial, and eventually a quiet, hopeless acceptance that life was never going to be the same again. Initially, the look in his eyes, which learned to blink once for no, and twice for yes, conveyed his feelings. Later, the respiratory technicians taught him how to speak on the expiratory breath. Slowly, painfully, he learned to use his voice then make sentences, laboriously exhaled in a halting staccato. It was draining for Wayne, and draining for his carers.

I took a holiday to Mexico for ten days to clear my head and come to terms with the emotional strain.

When I got back, I bounced back into the unit, all suntan and *joie de vivre*. I had bought a colourful Mexican puppet for Wayne, which I intended to hang on the metal halo that had been drilled into his skull to stabilize his poor, broken neck. I knew he'd love that puppet.

As I stepped up to his bedside, I saw that his chin was covered in a fluffy ginger stubble of young beard. As often happens with blondes, the attempt to grow a manly beard had produced something of a quite different colour.

'Wayne? What's going on? I don't like that much,' I burbled, without thinking. He shut down, eyes closed, and remained silent through my entire shift. I knew I had done something wrong, but wasn't really aware of what it could be.

Just before going off shift, I said, 'Wayne. Please tell me why you are upset.'

Slowly, with eyes still closed, haltingly, he said, 'All I can do for myself is refuse to be shaved. I thought I would do the only thing I could control, grow a beard, to show you just what I could do, for your return. And you do not like it.'

I wanted to cut out my tongue. I went home that evening knowing that Wayne had taught me a valuable lesson: think. Think before you speak.

*   *   *

Not only were intense relationships made between patient and carer within this intensive care unit, but also those of us working together on each shift became very good friends. Cecilia, always first to arrive on shift and last to leave, was a wonderfully caring nurse for whom nothing was too much trouble. She had a serenity about her that helped all of us, not just the patients in her care. She was married with two young children, and had a husband who was obviously a wonderful support for her. I learned much later that Cecilia had been a nun for fifteen years, which explained her aura of serenity.

While I was caring for Wayne, Cecilia nursed Rob, the young man in the bed opposite.

Rob was in his first year of law studies at the University of British Columbia. Not quite twenty years old, he had good looks, a bright intellect, and a shining future ahead of him. An only child, his parents—both successful lawyers—doted on him. The family lived in a beautiful house in the affluent suburbs of West Vancouver.

One weekend, Rob's parents left for a skiing trip to the Mammoth Mountain resort in

California, leaving their son with permission to have a party at the house. Rob's friends duly converged on the house, where cheap wine and marijuana were enjoyed. At one point, a dozen or so of the laughing young students crowded out of the sumptuous sitting room on to an adjoining balcony that looked on to the landscaped gardens just a few feet below.

Suddenly, the balcony gave way beneath them and the group collapsed in a giggling heap. They managed to disentangle themselves, however, and walked away—all except for Rob, who had been bottom of the pile of bodies. He had snapped his C3 vertebra, which caused paralysis from the shoulder blade downwards. Rob's girlfriend called emergency services, who brought him in to VGH. The only piece of luck to come his way that night was to have Cecilia assigned as his main carer.

As the weeks ticked by, Rob and Wayne each gradually tried to come to terms with their devastated lives. Rob's parents paid vast amounts of money for second and third medical opinions, but the answer was always the same. Over time, they even looked into the possibility of Rob's semen being salvaged and frozen, with a view to artificially inseminating his girlfriend to ensure that a grandchild could be born—an idea that sprang out of the frantic hope and the denial that is always present in the earliest days of such a tragedy, but was a new and unusual concept back in 1966 and not one we were entirely comfortable with. It all came to nothing, of course, and quietly grim reality settled in.

Rob's parents gently, but firmly, squeezed Mary out, his girlfriend, not wanting her life to be so drastically affected. Cecilia was wonderful at comforting and counselling this beautiful young woman who was trying to grapple with such a tragedy at the age of only twenty.

Rob had a dog called Timmy that he loved, and Timmy loved him right back. Rob wanted nothing more than to see his dog, a little terrier with bags of character. It was impossible to obtain permission for Timmy to be brought into the critical care unit so, with Christmas Day looming, Rob's parents began to work on the idea that their son could perhaps come home for a few hours on 25 December.

To take Rob away for the day, with all the risk that entailed to somebody with such devastating injuries and who needed to be permanently plugged into machines for his survival, was not something the hospital could officially sanction. Quite apart from any other consideration, they could open themselves up to litigation, a real fear among the medical profession. Over a period of weeks Rob's father painstakingly researched all avenues to get his son home for just a short while—long enough to share a Christmas meal with his parents and see Timmy.

Eventually, Cecilia and I, with a lawyer to witness our signatures, signed forms stating that we were acting against medical advice to assist in making this possible, and that the hospital could not be held responsible in any way. We were tacitly supported by junior medical and nursing staff. We knew that if anything went wrong and further endangered Rob's health or his life, we would most certainly be sacked, or even struck off the nursing register. Nonetheless, we were prepared to

55

take a calculated risk; to do what I guess today would be called 'going the extra mile'. We knew, as nurses, what that visit meant to Rob and his parents. That's what nursing is.

On Christmas Day, with enormous difficulty, Rob's father drove up in a van that had been, at great expense and following much research into what was available on the market, fitted with specially adapted ramps. With trepidation, we detached Rob from his suction machine and his respirator and quickly wheeled him up the ramps into the van, where we rapidly reconnected him to another respirator and a mobile suction machine. (He required frequent suction of the trachea as he was unable to swallow any secretions such as saliva or phlegm unaided—if not removed, these would slide into his lungs and kill him.)

To say this undertaking was stressful is an understatement, but we were all determined to give Rob one taste of normality. Wayne, too—cared for that day by the relief nurse—cheered us on, seeing the whole manoeuvre as bucking the system and making a break for freedom. Slowly Rob's father drove the van from downtown, across the Lionsgate Bridge to West Vancouver, carefully avoiding any sudden braking, potholes or awkward manoeuvres. Not easy in heavy traffic that Christmas Day.

Eventually we arrived at the house, where electric cables—snaking across the plush carpeting of the hallway and into the beautiful sitting room—were already waiting to connect respirator and suction machine. A huge, perfectly decorated Christmas tree twinkled with lights in the corner, and a log fire crackled in the hearth. Cecilia and I

56

quickly wheeled Rob into the house and connected his life-sustaining equipment once again.

Timmy the dog was sitting on the rug in front of the fire, in a scene that could have come straight from a traditional Christmas card. Rob's face lit up and his eyes shone with affection and happiness as soon as he saw Timmy.

But the dog, this sensitive little creature, backed away slowly and began to shiver. He knew something was not quite right with this picture. It looked like his Rob, but what were all these cables? What was that humming sound coming from the rear of the wheelchair? And why was Rob wrapped in a blanket, and not running towards him, slapping his thighs and calling his name as usual?

In that very moment, when his beloved dog realized something was terribly wrong, that split second of joy that had glowed in Rob's face disappeared. In that instant we saw him say a silent goodbye to his life.

We got through Christmas lunch somehow. Turkey, gravy, cranberry sauce and sweet potato had been liquidised for Rob, but he refused even a sip. We pulled crackers and laughed loudly, too loudly, in our efforts not to break down and weep. Then came the tortuous journey back to the hospital, and getting Rob back into the unit. Cecilia and I must have lost several pounds of weight in perspiration during the tense ordeal.

It was, we knew, Timmy who had shown Rob that his life would never be the same again. We had planned and prepared painstakingly for this day, anticipating every kind of problem that might be encountered on our patient's journey home.

But nobody had been prepared for the truthful, instinctive reaction of a beloved dog. We saw the effect on Rob, whose heart had been broken by the reunion that wasn't.

*　　*　　*

Two years later, long after I had left Vancouver General Hospital, Cecilia wrote to tell me that Wayne had died, having outlived Rob by a few months.

9

Cassiar

One of the enjoyable aspects of travelling to a new destination for the very first time is the way the bus or train station, or the airport departure lounge, takes on the spirit of the place to which you are headed.

So it was that, on 8 June 1966, I waved a cheery goodbye to friends at Vancouver airport and began my quest to discover wild Canada—the *real* Canada as I thought of it—and headed north towards the British Columbia/Yukon border.

Once in the departure lounge, the city-slicker sophistication of urban Vancouver fell away as I joined my fellow passengers headed north. The majority were men, whose rugged dress and grizzled looks spoke of many hours spent outdoors, no matter the weather. Jeans, cowboy boots and check shirts rubbed shoulders with

58

fringed suede jackets, braided hair and beaded headbands. But these were no hippies headed for San Francisco. These men were hard-working loggers, miners and hunters. A sprinkling of young Germans and Hungarians among them were headed to the mines that littered northwest British Columbia and the Yukon.

Slightly apart from the rest of us sat a small group of Indians. These were not the shambling, inebriated wrecks I had nursed in the emergency room, but fine-looking men, quiet and self-contained, with a purposeful air about them. Some wore moccasins, others the beaded mukluks I would learn about later. A few of the men had their families with them, and a handful of bright-eyed children played at their feet as they waited for the flight.

But, for all their dignity, the Indian group were still somehow not quite of the crowd. It would have been right to call them marginalized, though I didn't realize it then. (In truth, there was rather a lot about life that I didn't yet realise.)

I sat down next to another young woman who, it transpired, was also an English nurse and midwife. She was heading for the hospital in Whitehorse, capital of the romantic Yukon—think Gold Rush!—and I to the small hospital in the asbestos-mining town of Cassiar, deep in the mountains that marked the start of the Rocky Mountain ranges. We swapped notes and excitedly wondered what lay ahead of us.

In the 1960s, Canada was hungry for strong young men and women to go north, and for those equipped with skills, a strong back and a 'can do' attitude, there were employment opportunities

59

galore.

The flight to Watson Lake, via the river city of Prince George and the port of Prince Rupert in British Columbia, was uneventful but, as I gazed out the window, the sight of virgin forest stretching to infinity below me was spectacular. I had only ever imagined such sights during the bad times of my childhood, and now those dreams were the spur to the adventures that lay just ahead.

As the plane touched down in the Yukon, I knew I had made the right decision and that I was about to find 'the real thing'. Four of the immigrant Europeans on board were also new recruits for the asbestos mine at Cassiar, and the five of us were met by a wiry chap with a wrinkled, nut-brown face, who sucked on his curly-shaped home-made pipe and spat a lot. His extraordinarily pale grey eyes were sharp and intelligent and took in everything at a glance, even through the thick haze of tobacco smoke you would have thought would blind him. His gravity-defying trousers, several sizes too large, were held up by a long piece of rawhide knotted loosely and perched on his skinny hips. A too-large red and black plaid shirt completed the outfit, further adorned by several rows of coloured beads, a little black pouch, and a small, downy grey feather, all of which hung around his wizened neck. On his mop of silver-white hair, parted in the centre and worn in two braids that sat on his bony shoulders, rested a battered, dark green felt hat with unidentifiable bits of 'stuff' tucked into the leather band.

This was George.

The four hefty men with whom I was to share the journey stowed their luggage in the back of the large, beaten-up old truck that was to transport us; George effortlessly threw my suitcase and rucksack into the truck and we all piled in. The vehicle, which hardly seemed in the condition necessary for our rough ride, bounced along the dusty road to a hunting lodge-style restaurant nearby. There, George pulled up and strongly advised us to 'have a bite to eat, a beer and a piss'. It was a hot day and the cold beer went down easily. I chewed on a sandwich and tried not to notice that all the men in the place were staring soulfully at me, the only young woman in the place. The glassy eyes of the mounted moose and bear heads peering at me from the wood-panelled walls made me feel uncomfortable, and somehow a little sad.

I went outside and took a look around. Several large birds of prey circled overhead. George came out, spat a stream of tobacco-stained saliva into the dirt, squinted into the bright sky and said, 'Them's buzzards. Yep. Them sure is buzzards.'

I'd longed for something so genuinely different, and it certainly seemed like I was getting it!

We climbed back into the truck and began the ninety-mile journey to our destination, Cassiar, a company town of some 2,000 people. My fellow travellers were Joe and Des, Hungarians despite their names, and two Germans, Willy and Heinz. Judging by the hungry, approving looks I was getting from all four, I concluded—with some trepidation—that young women were at a premium in these parts.

As the truck bumped out of town, we passed a collection of signs nailed to tall, whitewashed posts. Each bore the name of a town or city, together with the mileage from Watson Lake to that town. Most were in the neighbouring USA, a few in Europe. George explained that these had been started during World War Two by homesick American GIs who came north in 1942 to build the Alaska Highway. I reckoned it was time a Welsh name was up there, and resolved to see to it.

We headed southwest, jolting along through spectacular scenery. With most of the journey still to come, and hitting spine-cracking potholed stretches of the dirt road from time to time, I was a bit alarmed to notice three shotguns and a rifle sat on gun racks behind the heads of the guys. I fervently hoped they weren't loaded, but I soon forgot all about them as the breathtaking country stunned all of us into awed silence.

Every so often, somebody would say something, but mostly we were hypnotised by the rugged grandeur of the mountains, towering behind sparkling lakes and rivers that shared the endless space with forests of tall fir trees and a profusion of beautiful wild flowers.

The entire road at that time was little more than a dusty, hard-packed dirt track. Every now and again, George had to pull over hard as a convoy of trucks bearing asbestos bound for Whitehorse, Alaska and the world thundered past and covered us in choking clouds of dust.

The pick-up had a large bull bar on the front. George explained that hitting a moose was like hitting a brick wall. 'Keep your eyes peeled, hon,' he cackled in his raspy, deep voice.

We didn't see moose that day, but we did see eagles: bald eagles and golden eagles, soaring high above us, and, to my huge excitement, a black bear ambled casually across the road.

'Hon, you don't ever—you hear me? —not ever stop and get out when you see a momma bear like that. Her cubs are nearby and she'll kill ya. Got it?'

I got it.

Something about George was bothering me, but I couldn't quite zero in on what it was. As we hurtled along at a juddering pace, I watched the pattern of ropey veins on the back of his hand as it wrestled with the vibrating gear stick next to my knee. My eyes moved to his surprisingly slender wrist, around which snaked a pretty silver and turquoise bangle, and suddenly it dawned on me: George was a woman!

During that simultaneously magnificent and hair-raising journey I learned that George, full name Georgina, was originally from Kent, 'the garden of England', where her father was a fruit farmer. When she was fifteen, her large family immigrated to Canada and settled in the Okanagan Valley, where they became successful peach farmers. Rebellious by nature, George married Paddy, a silver-tongued Irishman, and, to her parents' horror, they went off north to 'find their Eldorado'. George's voice softened when she spoke of Paddy, and how they had earned something of a living panning for gold together, but Paddy had been dead for fifteen years, killed in a road accident. The widowed George had chosen to stay on in the area, found a job as a jack of all trades in Cassiar, and made herself indispensable. It did occur to me that it would be wise to avoid the temptation to stay in Cassiar any longer than my one-year contract—much as I admired George, I wasn't ready to end up the same way! And I *did* admire her. No one told George what to do. She was a free spirit, who lived life dancing to her own tune. How great was that for a woman out in the wilds in those days?

*　　　*　　　*

As we drew closer to Cassiar, the sweeping landscape transformed into an alpine valley, fed by Good Hope Lake, where a seaplane was moored next to a wooden landing stage. This stood ready to transport casualties, or anyone suffering from an illness too serious for the small company hospital to manage, up to Whitehorse, some 300 miles north by air, where more medical specialists were based.

The valley floor was covered with a carpet of spring and early summer flowers; yellow arnica was growing abundantly alongside swathes of scarlet dwarf fireweed, the state flower of the Yukon; mauve crocus and the delicate white bog-star grew among shady trees, as did the deep blue Arctic lupin, which reminded me of our beloved bluebell woods back home in Wales. I felt a sudden pang of homesickness...

Approaching the town site, the road snaked around the base of an enormous pile of green stuff, the size of a small hill. This was my first glimpse of the 'tailings'—asbestos waste, whose sage-green colour was to become so familiar to me.

We bounced up to the Cassiar Company Hospital, a long, low white building with a few wooden steps leading up to a green front door. We came to a shuddering halt and Dr Stephen Navin and Valerie Melnyk RN came out to greet me warmly. George quickly dumped my luggage while the four guys wished me luck before being whisked off by George in a cloud of tobacco smoke to be assigned quarters in the long, low, log-built bunkhouses where single men were housed.

The small but perfectly designed hospital contained six beds, a delivery suite, and two cubicles leading off a main treatment room.

Dr Navin was an affable teddy bear of a man, with a head of thinning silvery hair and a thick white walrus moustache. His clinical practice might have been a little outdated—he treated almost everything with either mustard or kaolin poultices—but he sure proved a good man to have around in an emergency.

Over a welcome mug of strong tea, he asked me if I would mind plunging straight into a night shift because one of his nurses had suddenly been taken ill.

I was a little surprised. It was 4 p.m. and I had just tipped in from Vancouver, but hey, why not?

Valerie, also English, efficiently showed me the ropes. The night shift was usually straightforward, she said; maybe a few suturings following the odd drunken fight, and anyone requiring a few hours of observation could be admitted to one of the beds. No babies were due to be delivered for the next few days.

I was shown my quarters in a separate section towards the end of the hospital building. Two bedrooms with blacked-out windows, a large, airy sitting room, a spacious kitchen and a small bathroom. It was comfortable and cosy.

What I had not yet realized was that the sun barely set at that time of year. This was not called the Land of the Midnight Sun for nothing.

At around midnight, I went outside and sat on the top step. In the magical indigo twilight, breathing in the stillness of this beautiful place, I marvelled at the silhouette of the mountain ranges that crowded in on either side of the small hospital. The eerie stillness lasted maybe thirty minutes during which, if you looked carefully, you could glimpse the stars twinkling through the streaks of light already dawning in the sky.

This first, unexpected—and, if I'm honest, unwelcome—night shift contributed to the disorientation I experienced during the first two weeks of my new adventure. I reported for duty in daylight, worked in daylight, tried to get some sleep in daylight; and when I woke up, if I got any sleep at all, there it was again—the bright light of day. I had to keep persuading myself I was working the night shift!

Time became distorted, and when I began pulling day shifts, it took me some time to settle into sleeping in a normal sequence. Eventually my body clock was sorted, and I began to explore Cassiar.

* * *

The entire town of Cassiar had been built by the mining company for the purpose of mining asbestos. To all intents and purposes, it was run by the company and the men and women who lived there were employed by, or connected in some way, to the Cassiar Mining Company. Cassiar today is a ghost town, but in 1966 it was a vibrant and thriving little place.

The welfare of the company's employees was well taken care of. When I made my first real tour of the town, I discovered a bank, a post office, a general store, a lively school and three churches of varying denominations. An RCMP (Royal Canadian Mounted Police) officer took care of upholding the law of the land.

I was soon approached to see if I was willing to act as a female chaperone, in the event of there being a female prisoner in the cells. I said I would, was fingerprinted and screened, and found myself working quite a few night shifts chaperoning the mainly Indian women locked up for various alcohol-related fracas. This is where I learned that a bottle of Scotch could buy a miner a 'squaw' for the night. How cruelly casual were the thoughtless put-downs. It seemed that these people who lived on the fringes were assumed to be unemployable, drunken irrelevances, barely deserving or worthy of Canadian citizenship.

A small percentage of senior company personnel were allowed to bring their wives, but for the most part employees were unmarried men of varying nationalities. The few single women, who were mainly teachers and nurses, were under pressure. This was a new experience for me. I had two brothers and tended to look at most young men as brothers. Always a smiley, friendly and open person, I soon learned to 'shut down' a bit.

When a young, single woman is surrounded by 2,000 healthy single men, body language has to change. If you smiled at someone, rumours that you were obviously having an affair with that person spread like a bushfire. It took me a while to cotton on to this phenomenon, which was quite new to me. Also new to me was the discovery that it was usually the other single women who were spreading the rumours. So much for sisterhood ...

Almost everything about Cassiar was new territory for me. In both its best and worst aspects, though, the life there proved a good training ground for my nursing experience in Vietnam, which was to follow—sooner than I could ever have imagined. There the ratio of single young women to single young men was to be so much greater, and a hell of a lot more pressurized!

A large recreation hall showed movies three times a week; the well-stocked library was very popular, and cerebral games like chess, bridge, draughts and dominoes were well patronized, particularly by Europeans; while badminton, table tennis, pool and soccer were popular with everyone. There was also a huge curling rink. I learned to play this relatively unknown Scottish game and became reasonably proficient, joining the hospital team and thoroughly enjoying it. I am still the only person I know who watches and yells support for this event during the Winter Olympics.

The steep hill to the rear of the hospital had a ski lift. This was where I was able to sit on the back step of my living quarters, strap on my skis, snow-plough a few feet to the rope tow, and be hauled up the steep slope. I learned the hard way not to attempt a downhill ski in temperatures of minus thirty. My face took a battering in that winter climate, but I learned also to use snow shoes, a much gentler way to cover ground in such raw temperatures. I loved the outdoor life, and embraced it all with joy.

Having put my salmon-poaching experience well

behind me, I found myself again learning to fish, this time legitimately and seriously. The nearby lakes and rivers were teeming with grayling, trout and the familiar plump, gleaming salmon!

I saw dozens of moose, either standing sleepily knee-deep in a lake, or blundering across a track. These magnificent creatures always took my breath away. And bears, so many bears: brown, black, and—the most scary—the grizzly. The rugged beauty of the land around Cassiar was a great place to see Canadian wildlife, and I loved it all. I learned to be careful when choosing a campsite, though—never anywhere near wild strawberry patches. Bears love them as much as we do.

* * *

The high-grade, green, long-fibred chrysotile asbestos was used in the heat shields on NASA space capsules, and in the astronauts' space suits. There were no health concerns during this mid-1960s period, and the opencast mining town of Cassiar prospered and vibrated with life.

Twice a day the loud warning siren reverberated around the mountain ranges and throughout the town as explosives were detonated, loosening the pay dirt. Over the years, giant terraces were gouged into the McDame mountain range, scarring the natural beauty of this beautiful place.

The ore was trucked down, at that time, to the mill 2,000 feet below, where the asbestos was crushed repeatedly, 'fluffing' up the commercially valuable fibres, which were then graded by length and compressed into 45-kilo bags, then trucked to

Whitehorse. From there, they were carried on the famous White Pass narrow-gauge railway to Skagway, Alaska, and shipped south to Vancouver from where they were sent to all points across the globe.

By the early 1970s, health concerns about the effects of inhaling asbestos began to infiltrate the public consciousness, and the alarm was raised internationally. By 1992 the asbestos industry had been bankrupted; Cassiar's inhabitants left and the equipment was auctioned off.

10

The Real Thing

Over the coming years, as my nursing travels took me further afield to other countries and cultures, I came to learn more than I would ever have wished to know about the ruthless pattern of cruel disregard and cultural destruction waged against the indigenous people of various countries. Sadly, certain of these countries were—and still are—members of the British Commonwealth.

It was in Cassiar that I came to know something about the native North American, but it was only several years later that I fully grasped the extent of a horror story that shames us all.

After my early encounters with Canadian Indians in the emergency room at Vancouver General, my first impressions were hardly balanced. Those men and women, shambling wrecks existing amid the human detritus on the streets of the city's skid row, were brought in regularly by the ambulance services or police. We did what we could to help them but, with only a pitifully short time available, and within the limitations of a clinical setting, it was clear that we were fighting a losing battle. What made the situation even worse was the widespread belief that the Indian was a useless, drunken, unemployable creature, hardly fit to be part of Canadian society.

This attitude, which I'm sorry to say was not uncommon even among medical staff, was constantly reinforced by the procession of sorry sights in the ER and on the streets.

No one, it seemed, was willing to take responsibility for the history and treatment of these early Canadians. The words used so casually—'squaw', 'chug' or 'wagon burner'—were commonplace insults, equivalent in their effect to calling a black American 'nigger', or a black South African 'kaffir'.

That, then, had been my sorry introduction to a once proud people whose culture and land had been treated with disrespect. Powerless to fend off the greedy encroachment of white civilisation, the Indians had long since been herded into reserves, created by the colonisers of that vast and beautiful country. There, they eked out an existence as best they could, while their traditions and very identity were gradually eroded.

But while I was instinctively uncomfortable with the attitude that prevailed in the hospital, and in Vancouver's white society in general, I knew little about the situation and have to admit to turning at least half a blind eye as I continued on my travels.

A few miles outside of Cassiar, on the banks of one of the mountain lakes, was a settlement of a few dozen Indians. Some of the canoes moored at the wooden jetty on the lake were painted with traditional patterns, their paddles carved with scroll designs suggesting fish and eagles. Their area was known as The Village and they too were permitted to use the hospital facilities. The cluster of log cabins, off the dirt road leading towards the mining community, always had gaggles of runny-nosed children playing outside. Nailed to the doorposts of most cabins were various collections of delicately carved pendants made from bone or antler, sometimes jade, found nearby. Carved goat-horn spoons of various sizes hung from rawhide strips; feathers and beaded pouches fluttered in the summer breeze. Some doorways had whittled patterns worked into the logs.

Moose antlers sat bleaching on the roofs in the hot summer sunshine, and animal skins were usually to be seen stretching and drying on wooden frames, to be sold later up in Whitehorse. The Indians had their own smoke houses, where fish was preserved for the long, hard winter months ahead. Historically these people, who were members of the Tahltan tribe, were respected among other tribes for their hunter-gatherer skills.

Several of the men in The Village made a good living taking American hunters on forays into the surrounding bush, helping them to bag moose or bear, or to catch themselves fish that really were 'this big'.

A few of the men were employed in the mill and were known to be strong, reliable workers, but generally they kept themselves to themselves. It was through meeting their shy womenfolk in the hospital that I began to learn something of their traditional medicines.

They had their own village shaman, who took care of most illnesses. He also set the bones of simple fractures, splinting them with small branches whittled down to size and held in place with binding cut from animal hides. Shirts were ripped up to make slings, or were torn into strips, boiled in a pot over the campfire, and used to bandage up wounds or burns. Minor accidents were treated within their community, and most normal deliveries of bouncing babies were taken care of by the women.

They came to the hospital only if something was worrying them, often needing nothing more than a little reassurance. It was as though white man's medicine was nibbling at the edges of their centuries-old herbal treatments, and beginning to erode confidence in their healing properties.

Or maybe it was beginning to be seen as moving with the times, possibly being more 'fashionable'. That, I have learned, is how the slow infiltration of doubt in traditional values starts: breast-feeding gives way to bottle-feeding, bringing its own problems: bottles have to be sterilised adequately, money is needed to pay for powdered milk, and the benefits of breast milk are lost.

As the months went by and the Indian mothers learned to trust me, I was able to visit The Village regularly, and often sat chatting over a steaming mug of willow-bark tea. I always approached one

73

of the elders, Melvin Pete or Larry Muskrat—yes, even their Indian names were now private to them—to ask permission to enter their space.

I rarely saw an infected wound or burn coming from The Village. Something called 'spruce pitch' was commonly used to pack into, or over, any serious break in the skin. The bark of the spruce bush was carved off with a knife and chewed until it formed a soft cud. The saliva was spat onto one of the boiled cloths, which was then placed over the wound, burn or scald, and the 'cud' packed firmly over the area. I often saw a nasty third-degree burn several days after the initial accident, but never an infection. Rarely were antibiotics required following this treatment.

One day Melvin Pete brought in his daughter, Mary, with what had been a nasty breast abscess. It had been lanced with a knife that was held over a flame and, the pus released, the remaining crater was packed with spruce pitch. The entire area was clean and required no further treatment other than clean dressings over the next few days. Mary's baby continued to breast-feed quite happily for six months afterwards.

In springtime, the women would harvest copious amounts of pussy willow to manufacture another effective treatment. The delicate twigs with their silky buds were boiled furiously in a large pot until the liquid was a brownish-yellow colour. Then the liquid was strained and bottled, and kept year-round to take for menstrual cramps, intestinal cramps when gastric upsets threatened, and even to dull labour pains. Despite its bitter taste, it appeared to be very effective, and one of the British nurses at the hospital swore by it.

Another settlement, smaller and half a mile closer to Cassiar and tucked away in the trees, housed another—and distressingly different—group. That was where most of our Indian patients came from. Vicious, drunken fights were commonplace. These were the folk considered as being 'on the wrong side of the tracks' and they were in a sorry state. Illicit booze was always on the go here, and the area was frequented by the rougher element from among the single miners in camp. I was forewarned never to go into this area, and I was reminded of Hastings Street in Vancouver.

The women from this place were reduced to allowing themselves to be used and abused. Their cabins and canvas tents were unkempt, surrounded by garbage and crying children. The occasional suspicious death occurred at times. I was asked to chaperone incarcerated females many times during my year in Cassiar, as were other nurses and teachers. It was always sad to see these women begging for alcohol or cannabis, anything to blot out their immediate pain. When in the grip of the DT's, they tore at their skin, drawing blood in a desperate effort to gouge out the imaginary creepy-crawlies they thought they saw writhing beneath their skin. Self-harming was the danger and I, along with the other chaperones, were there to offer a little human kindness or, more likely, to prevent a hanging suicide, which had occurred in the past. Occasionally the shaman was allowed to visit to call up the spirits in an attempt to provide some relief.

At three in the morning on one particular night in the depths of winter, one of the incarcerated women began to sing in her own tongue. Her voice was haunting; crystal clear and full of pain. It made the hair stand up on the back of my neck, and I still recall it now, vividly and tearfully, as it resonates with me down through the years, to my little cottage in Devon. How could such beauty descend into such desolation?

What are we doing to each other? I thought then, and I think now.

*   *   *

It was at this time, 1966/67, that the new birth-control pill began to be dispensed.

Some of the women continually asked us for help 'to stop babies coming', but this was a man's world so any undertaking involving contraception had to be discussed with the women's husbands or partners. Such discussions were generally short, sharp and unproductive.

But the women, used and abused by some of the miners as well as by their own menfolk, needed protecting from themselves, as did the babies they bore every eight months or so, regular as clockwork. It was here that I first saw babies born with Foetal Alcohol Syndrome (FAS).

Born prematurely, with folds of wrinkled skin hanging loosely from their tiny, scraggy buttocks and arms, they looked like little old men. There was no rosy chubbiness in their world; rye whisky had coursed through their damaged systems while in their mother's womb. Always small for their age, those who survived usually went on to have behavioural and learning difficulties, impaired memory and a host of deficiencies. We tried to help the women prevent pregnancies, and the new miracle pill seemed like the answer. One small pill a day. How convenient.

But this was a step too far for Bluebell, Primrose, Lucy, and others.

These women would pitch up at the hospital every few days 'for more of them fucking pills, Sister'.

'Where are those I gave you last week?' I would ask.

'Well, Sister, I gave two to Primrose, three to Mary and six to Florence. Then Mary gave one of hers to Lizzie ...' Who the heck knew who had taken what?

Eventually we decided to get the defaulters to come to the hospital every day to be given their pill on the spot where we could watch them swallow it. That lasted all of a few days as appointments were either forgotten or slept through.

Then we tried IUDs—the coil. That was definitely not popular. 'The men don't like it, Sister.' And if the men didn't like it, well, then it was not going to happen!

And so it went on. The sickly babies kept coming, interspersed with their hapless mothers' various gynaecological emergencies every eight months.

The kitten-like faces of these tiny mites, their eyes screwed up against the light, their saddle noses and, later, ridged Hutchinson's teeth, spoke of syphilis.

Sadly, even today, those trapped on 'the wrong side of the tracks' in any such community, wherever it may be, are usually the most visible, and therefore wrongly judged to be 'typical' of whichever social group they are seen to represent by a seemingly uncaring, short-sighted society.

11

All that Glisters ...

The Cassiar Company Hospital had been set up to deal with the health and welfare of all company employees, the majority of whom were Canadians and Europeans—and white.

Our team—one doctor and four nurses—were kept busy attending to school health, vaccination programmes, ante-natal and post-natal care, births, and tending trauma and first-aid cases. Last, but very far from least, we carried out three-monthly chest X-rays and lung function tests on all those working inside the mill. Health concerns about the dangers of asbestos had not yet surfaced, and I never saw anybody wearing protective masks anywhere on site.

During the short summers, recreational activities centred on water sports on the surrounding lakes, which led to an occasional near drowning. One day, a rather well-upholstered German wife, face down on a stretcher, was carried into the hospital by a group of men. She pointedly refused to speak with her husband, who sat on the steps outside puffing on a cigarette and waiting.

His wife's ample backside was barely covered by

her bright red swimsuit, which stretched across her enormous buttocks, one cheek of which had a thick lint pad taped to it. It turned out that he had been teaching her to water-ski at the lake. She had been sitting on the end of the wooden jetty, feet placed firmly into the water-skis, her hands gripping the tow bar fixed by a long tow rope to the speedboat, when he gunned the engine. The boat took off at speed, her bottom scraped along the rustic planking of the jetty, and a huge sliver of wood embedded itself deep into her buttock.

She was still fuming at the indignity, and as I injected local anaesthetic into her dimpled flesh I could hear her husband and his mates roaring with laughter outside. When I was eventually able—with some difficulty—to remove the offending wedge of jetty, it measured a good six by four inches! Was that what I'd gone to Cassiar for, I asked myself wryly . . .

During the long winter months, when daylight was scarce and temperatures remained at forty below zero, men would come in with ice burns, sometimes with frostbite, but the biggest problem was chest infections. The log cabins and trailers where the workers and their families lived were oil-fired and overheated, and the crystalline air outside could freeze the lungs. Children in particular were vulnerable. Alcohol abuse brought its own grief and drunken fights were not unusual at weekends. I was well able to perfect my suturing techniques here.

*　　*　　*

My year in this remote part of wild Canada passed in a whirl of camping, trekking, fishing and revelling in observing animals and birds in the wild. I improved my skiing and marvelled at my first sight of the aurora borealis. These vast curtains of coloured light dancing across the night skies left me breathless with wonder at the magical sight. I made several good friends in the Indian community: Johnny Jack took me ice fishing; Joe Dennis taught me to gut fish caught in the sparkling lakes and rivers skilfully and cleanly; Mary Pete showed me how stuffing several layers of newspaper and cardboard inside the beaded moccasins she made for me kept the freezing ground at bay for several hours when walking on packed snow and ice.

Twice I escorted patients by seaplane up to Whitehorse, and on several occasions I paid a social visit to the Yukon capital, where Ruth was nursing at the general hospital.

For the annual February Sourdough Rendezvous, which celebrates the Klondike Gold Rush of the late 1890s, the entire town dresses in costume—think Charlie Chaplin! I spent weeks sewing myself an amazing scarlet and black outfit, with the words of Miss Whitfield, my domestic science teacher back in Wales, ringing in my ears: 'Anne Watts, a blind man on a galloping horse can sew better than this!' Hah! I'd show her. The finished product had a huge bustle and a low-cut bodice edged in black lace, and I wore it to the White Horse Inn dance on the Saturday night, looking like something of a cross between Diamond Lil and Ma Walton!

The inn had been transformed for the occasion

into an 1890s bar. Men wearing striped shirts, green visors and sweaty, intense expressions played poker at green baize-covered tables. The bartenders took the mirrors off the wall each time a staged fight broke out, hanging them back again when said inebriated clients were slung out of the saloon doors into the street! There the RCMP officers, on duty but dressed like Keystone Cops, picked them up from the sidewalk and locked them into portable cells parked conveniently outside.

Halfway through an energetic polka, someone trod on the hem of my dress, ripping out the entire bustle!

My gallant partner, Des (one of the dishy Hungarians I had arrived with back in June), covered my blushes and guided me outside, where the sub-zero February temperature bit into my exposed backside. I had to beat a fast retreat to change into jeans and shirt, after which Des and I returned to the inn and happily danced the night away.

The person who stole the show that night was George, our trusty driver. She fitted right into the scene, leaning against a wall in the corner, quietly watching everyone and puffing away contentedly on her pipe. George had no need to dress in period costume; she always did fit right in by just being herself. I have never seen a white woman drink so much alcohol and still appear to be stone-cold sober.

The next day, I rescued my reputation by coming second in the Ladies' Snow Shoe race. I still have that blue rosette and am proud of it. The other eight contestants were all Indian women

81

and girls. I felt I did Wales proud up there in the frozen Yukon.

And I also made good on my promise to myself to make sure that a Welsh place name joined the mainly American signs at Watson Lake.

Llanfairpwllgwyngyllgogerychwyrndrobwyllllantysiliogogogoch—yes, really—is a small town on the island of Anglesey in North Wales, not far from where I spent the first seventeen years of my life, and I was determined that name would go up there.

The sheriff at Watson Lake, from whom I had to secure permission to hang the sign, thought I had taken leave of my senses. He just guffawed loudly, suggesting I have a drink over at the bar and I'd soon feel better. I tried to convince him that this was a genuine place name, meaning 'the church of St Mary in a hollow of white hazel near a rapid whirlpool close to St Tysilio's church near the red cave' all in the Welsh language. But the sheriff would have none of it.

The carpenters in the Cassiar workshop fell about laughing at my attempts to teach them to say it, and said their biggest problem would be that they had insufficient letter Ls to form such a name. I'd show them!

I wrote to my father for a postcard displaying the name clearly. He sent me two postcards, which finally convinced the incredulous sheriff.

'Goddam it. What kinda horseshit name is that? Go on, girl, get on with it,' he laughed, and we set to work.

A twelve-foot-long plank of cedar wood was given several coats of black weatherproofed paint and then the name was stencilled on, using large

82

capital letters sprayed on with bright orange paint. The finished sign, once dry, was then varnished over—twice. It looked good. Incomprehensible to everyone except me, but it looked good.

Next day, a truck led by a convoy of jeeps and rough-terrain vehicles trundled the ninety miles to Watson Lake. Accompanied by great ceremony and the drinking of copious amounts of beer, the sign was nailed firmly to four posts. George managed to laugh uproariously, spit tobacco juice and puff on her pipe simultaneously. I never could figure out how she did that without choking to death. The bemused sheriff watched the whole thing, stetson tipped back on his head as he scratched his forehead, muttering, 'Goddam limeys! I don't know 'bout this.'

That sign stayed up there for years.

* * *

I travelled into Alaska on the amazing narrow-gauge White Pass train, which takes you through the Chilkoot Pass. This follows the route taken by prospectors flooding up from California to seek their fortune in gold. They were unprepared for the bitter winter and many perished. The train stopped at Dead Horse Gulch, looking out over spectacular scenery from an elevation of 3,500 feet. Here, a bronze sculptured memorial marks the spot where the remains of some 300 starving packhorses, laden with supplies, had perished in the arctic conditions.

There was not much in Skagway in 1966. I stayed overnight at the only hotel, a timbered affair where the bar was crowded with men, and the lock on my bedroom door was broken. I dragged the chest of drawers across the door, lay on the bed fully clothed and barely slept a wink all night.

Next morning I took a walk up the one main street and into a pretty birch wood. A little way along a small path, I came across a small cemetery. Sunshine dappled through the trees onto graves marked either with wooden crosses or boulders. Most bore the names and ages of babies and young children, and some the names of their young mothers buried with them. All of them, buried between 1897 and 1899, had died in the icy winter months, for which they were so ill prepared.

Gold fever had claimed many lives.

I took the overnight ferry to Juneau and watched the sun set and rise over a two-hour span of silent celestial beauty.

In 1867 the United States had bought Alaska from the Russians for seven million dollars. Believing that the territory—a distant colony, difficult to supply—was nothing but a frozen, inhospitable wasteland, the Russians must have thought they'd struck a really good bargain. I can only wonder how their decision-makers felt when the Klondike Gold Strike exploded in 1896!

Juneau was the state capital, and a stranger capital I have yet to see. With a 1966 population of some 9,000 hardy people, the whole town was built up the steep-sided mountain that dominated the narrow sound. From Juneau I took a helicopter ride to see the mighty Mendenhall Glacier. With difficulty, I walked across the uneven surface of this river of pale blue ice, 3,000 feet thick in places, and three miles wide at its widest point. I spoke to a small group of students from UBC (University of British Columbia, Vancouver) who were camped out on the glacier—studying, of all things, insect life! I never knew there were insects on a glacier ...

I flew back to Whitehorse later that day, en route to Cassiar, having learned something of the courageous pioneering spirit of those who settled such a starkly beautiful but unforgiving part of the globe. I returned to work feeling very privileged.

*　　　*　　　*

My time in Cassiar was marked indelibly by two events from back home in Britain—one joyous, one stark tragedy.

On 30 July 1966, with so many Europeans among the workforce, the football World Cup Final taking place at Wembley Stadium in far-away London was causing great excitement.

Union Jacks and German flags flew from bunkhouses and trailers and feverish bets were placed. I set my alarm for 5 a.m. to listen to the game on the radio.

The miners had decided that the citizens of whichever country lost the match would buy the whole camp a drink.

I ran up and down the corridor of the small hospital following Geoff Hurst's hat-trick of goals; the town went nuts, and it's the only time in my life I have ever had a beer with breakfast.

The Germans had one hell of a bar bill to settle that day ...

*　　　*　　　*

85

Almost three months later, at 9.15 a.m. local time on 21 October 1966, the children of Pantglas Junior School in Aberfan, South Wales, brought their morning assembly to a close with the hymn 'All Things Bright and Beautiful'. They were making their giggling way to their classrooms when, preceded by an eerie silence, a roaring noise suddenly filled their ears: it was the ugly sound of a 700-foot-high heap of sludge and waste, dislodged by two weeks of rain, sliding down the mountainside, burying the school and twenty private houses.

In total, 144 people died that day. Five were teachers at the school and 116 of them were young children.

When we learned of this tragedy via radio bulletins, I witnessed first-hand the immediate, heartfelt reaction of one mining community to the devastation in another.

Though separated by the Atlantic Ocean and an entire continent, the sentiments of the two communities were as one; the special connection felt by miners the world over was plain to see. Immediately, and spontaneously, with the news still being relayed, caps were passed around and people donated their hard-earned dollars to help the stricken community.

I was deeply touched, and learned something valuable that day about empathy, generosity and a true sense of belonging to the human family.

A disaster fund was set up in Wales to aid the physical and emotional regeneration of a shocked community, where an entire generation had been wiped out. Over time, a village hall was built, memorials were raised but, most importantly, if belatedly, all remaining waste tips in the area were removed.

I could never again look at that pile of asbestos tailings dominating the entrance to Cassiar without thinking of the children of Aberfan.

12

The Voyage Home

The grip of the Yukon winter melted into the slush and mud of early spring. With the sun riding ever higher in the sky, lengthening precious daylight hours from winter's three to summer's twenty-one, the celestial clock reminded me that my stay in Cassiar was approaching a whole twelve months. As the earth warmed up, the beautiful flowers that had welcomed me to this part of Canada a year earlier miraculously popped up again. Soft purple prairie crocus on open ground and the rose-purple fairy slipper, which preferred the shade of the spruce forest, signalled that my time in the north was drawing to a close.

My plan had always been to stay for a year and, observing the women who had been snapped up by lonely miners—many again heavily pregnant and with toddlers playing at their feet in the cramped trailers that were their homes—I knew I needed to move on.

Des tried to change my mind. He was a great guy, we shared a friendship that soon erupted into a passionate affair, as happens when you're young and high on life. It ran its natural course, as these things do, and I was not ready for the trap of domesticity to stop me in my tracks. There was way too much more to be learned about the world.

The day before I left, I went down to The Village to say goodbye to my friends. Mary Pete shyly gave me a pair of mukluks, warm and comfortable, that came up to my mid-calf. She had made them herself from the softest skin of a curly-horned mountain sheep hunted by her father Melvin Pete. A wide band of brown rabbit fur trimmed the boots, and their scuts provided for two pom-poms that hung down the sides from a strip of rawhide. Decorating the front of each boot were tiny beads of red and turquoise.

The boots smelled strongly of animal, and of campfires, but I was thrilled with my gift. In turn, since Mary had always loved my perfectly ordinary pair of sunglasses, I presented them to her. Hardly a fair swap, but she was very pleased and excitedly ran to show them off to some of the other women.

Melvin Pete gave me one of the spoons he had carved from goat's horn and a firm handshake. Then he turned and walked down to the nearby lake, from where he gave me a wave before paddling away in his canoe.

I still have both gifts, and treasure them. The mukluks never quite lost their distinctive smell, despite my hanging them outside for long periods over the coming years, but their faint musk brought back instant and vivid memories of The Village and my friends.

I remember wondering whether, should I ever return to Cassiar at some time in the future, I would find indigenous people employed as nurses, doctors, teachers, in Northern British Columbia and the Yukon. Perhaps a Cree pilot would fly me to Whitehorse, and the sheriff at Watson Lake or the RCMP officer might be members of the Tahltan band in the area.

George drove me to Watson Lake to catch the Vancouver flight. Her teeth were clamped firmly on her pipe as usual, but she removed it long enough to roar with laughter as we bowled past 'my' Welsh sign, where a group of tourists were taking photographs of it. We had a last beer together in the saloon before we parted, and I asked if there was anyone she wanted me to say hello to in England.

'Thanks, hon,' she replied, 'but no. Ain't no one there will remember me, and I don't remember 'em neither.'

She shook my hand, hesitated, then gave me a big bear hug before turning, spitting in the dirt and strolling off to meet the next batch of fresh-faced arrivals.

I hoped to revisit this beautiful area, and to see how much more of the mountain ranges had been carved up to feed the hungry market for the high-grade asbestos.

*   *   *

Back in Vancouver, two weeks passed in a whirlwind of goodbye parties, packing, repacking, and sealing up the mukluks in two plastic bags to keep the smell from invading the rest of my belongings. My sister Joan, who had been working as a nanny in Vancouver, came to the end of her one-year contract, and my friend Ruth had resigned from Whitehorse hospital, so the three of us set sail for home together, travelling on the modern ocean liner, the SS *Canberra* (which, many years later, would see service in the Falklands War).

Being on board the *Canberra* felt a very leisurely way to move between continents. The ship had started from Sydney, so there were many Australian passengers, making their way to Britain and Europe. The younger ones were out for adventure, but many of the families appeared to be British: those who had travelled out in the 1950s, encouraged and assisted by the Australian Government to seek a new and better life than post-war austerity Britain was offering. However, some of the 'Ten-pound Poms'—referring to their assisted passage to Australia—had become disillusioned or homesick and, unable to settle, were returning home.

The voyage from Vancouver to Southampton took thirty days, including brief stops at various points en route where we had the option to go ashore for a few hours. This was July 1967, and our first port of call was San Francisco. We didn't know it then, but this was the period remembered now as the Summer of Love.

After a delicious meal at Fisherman's Wharf the three of us headed off cheerfully to stroll in San Francisco's famous Golden Gate Park. Once in the park, to our stunned amazement we found ourselves in the middle of a mass of naked hippies—and I'm talking stark! Daisy chains and coloured beads garlanded their heads and, more unusually, were woven decoratively through pubic hair. The heady smell of cannabis wafted around us as bodies writhed on the grass in what I assumed was ecstasy, though it was difficult to tell. People strummed guitars and beat out rhythms on bongo drums and—though I find it hard to believe now—I was actually quite shocked at the spectacle. I felt protective of Joan, and needed to get her away from all this before we were roped in to something we might regret. My younger sister, however, was unfazed and to this day laughs at the memory of my reaction.

The saying goes that if you remember the '60s, you weren't there. Well, I *was* there, and I've never forgotten!

* * *

Negotiating the Panama Canal was definitely a highlight of the voyage. Traversing this massive waterway, which covers fifty miles between the Pacific and Atlantic oceans, took eight or nine hours. Three sets of locks raised and lowered shipping eighty feet, and I could hardly believe the ease and speed with which our 45,000-ton ship was dispatched, as though it were just a cork bobbing on the water.

Sailing through the Caribbean, then across the Atlantic, and finally into the English Channel, we could sense the excitement of those returning home. The fun-loving Aussies had spent the most time on board, some eight weeks, and were more than ready to leave behind their cabin fever. When Joan and I caught our first glimpse of England, we became quite emotional; the moment gave me a sudden poignant insight into how my father, and thousands of others like him, must have felt when they returned after many months at sea, particularly during the war years.

*   *   *

We disembarked at Southampton and boarded a train for London, where we took our leave of Ruth and travelled on up to North Wales. It was a far cry from Northern Canada, which rapidly receded into a 'did it really happen?' dream as Joan and I were immediately put to work. It was mid-August, the holiday season, and the hotel was full. The excitement of returning home rapidly faded into the drudgery of working all hours cleaning, washing dishes and waitressing.

This couldn't go on for too long, of course. I was pondering my next move when I came across the advertisement that would entirely change my life and my perceptions. Placed by the Save the Children Fund, it asked for nurses for a children's rehabilitation centre in Qui Nhon, Vietnam.

Within weeks, I found myself catapulted into Saigon, en route to Qui Nhon where I spent my first tour of duty, fifteen months, experiencing at first hand the tragedies of the Vietnam War.

The years 1967 to 1970 are what I call my 'growing up' years. Nothing can prepare you for what you see when staring into the face of war, any war. This particular war raged on around me, in the coastal town of Qui Nhon, and later during my time in the beautiful central highlands town of Kontum.

The faces I was looking into were those of babies, toddlers, teens and mothers. Bloodied, tear-stained, napalmed and lost—all needing a big hug. Nurses are good at hugs.

There were proud young soldiers, pumped up and ready to kick ass for their country, whether that be Vietnam or the USA. One half-fighting from below ground, the others bombing from above. Just where was the elusive Ho Chi Minh Trail? B-52s and defoliants did not solve the enigma. But an awful lot of people got hurt.

Failed diplomacy and poor political decision making clouded by poor vision can only end in chaos. It did, and it still does today.

But the little miracles of healing, compassion and courage that I witnessed at every turn are what I wrote about in *Always the Children*. I met extraordinary people in amazing places, all of us sharing our common humanity at a basic human level.

Vietnam taught me that we *can* make a difference. Part of being human is to roll up our sleeves and take an active part in repairing harm. Each and every one of us is able to do whatever we can, wherever we are and with whatever we have. There is a magnificence that exists in all of us, wherever we are.

Despite the stultifying heat, the terrifying military machine and the damage being wreaked around me, I matured, honed my nursing skills and knew that these lessons would stay with me for the remainder of my life. It is clear to me what war is—and what it is not. It is not medals, marching bands and glorious victory. It is fear, chaos, mistakes and weapons that mutilate and kill. There are no winners, only losers.

I came to realise that, while uniforms, languages

93

and landscape may change, the pursuit of power and the disastrous lack of political vision remained the same.

13

Fashionable London

November 1970. I had returned from my two tours of duty in Vietnam, safe but not completely sound. My work at Dr Patricia Smith's Minh Quy Mission Hospital, at Kontum in the central highlands, had been brought to a screeching halt by a severe bout of falciparum malaria that had completely floored me.

Back home and still feeling weak, I found the cool, clean air of Wales deliciously life-affirming, and my appetite quickly returned thanks to my father's insistence that I eat lots of liver and dark-green cabbage 'to perk me up and redden the blood'. A US Army hospital pathologist had given me two glass smears and a copy of the lab report to give my doctor back home. These proved my father absolutely right in prescribing his iron-rich cure—my haemoglobin had sunk to a shocking low.

The healthy diet loaded with iron soon ensured my haemoglobin levels bounced up, but the repeated appearance of liver and cabbage on my dinner plate was something I began to dread—until I thought of my childhood in the 1940s and '50s. In those days the treatment for pretty much any ailment was an 'opening medicine'. Didn't matter what the problem was, Father would say, 'What you need is a good opening medicine,' and line up us children for a disgusting dose of syrup of figs or, worse, castor oil. God, how we hated that stuff! Liver and cabbage was easier.

After a month or so I felt much stronger and was able to help with the frantic business of Christmas in the hotel. But my brothers and sisters were no longer there, and I missed them. Joan was undergoing nurse training in the Royal Air Force; my sister Susan was busy at home in Norfolk with her husband and two beautiful children; brother Hugh was still in the Royal Air Force, recently returned from Singapore but no longer living at home; and my brother Paul was newly married and also living elsewhere.

I not only missed my siblings but also my work. My stint in Vietnam, its pleasures as well as its daily horrors, began to seem a far-away dream, but my heart was still in Southeast Asia, and every instinct told me that I would go back there as soon as I could. Meanwhile, I knew I wasn't about to make a career of helping run the family hotel, and I set about finding another nursing position.

*   *   *

Christmas 1970 came and went, and shortly after the New Year I moved down to London to take up a position as a senior nurse in the emergency room of St Stephen's Hospital. This large teaching hospital (now replaced by the Chelsea and Westminster) sat on the Fulham Road, parallel to the fashionable and happening King's Road, Chelsea.

I took up residence in a rented apartment at 345 King's Road, along with four friends who, together, made up a mini League of Nations: Rene was a schoolteacher from Cape Town; Norma, strikingly beautiful but cripplingly shy, was a Jamaican nurse; Peggy, also a nurse, was a down-to-earth Aussie from Victoria who called a spade a bloody shovel; and chirpy Mary, another schoolteacher, hailed from Canada.

Between the five of us we could just about come up with the monthly rent of £100. We were blissfully unaware that we were living bang in the middle of social history, but I guess one never knows that at the time; you are where you are, and you just get on with life. And life in Chelsea brought me eighteen months that I remember with fondness and joy.

While my shifts at work demanded discipline and focus, time off duty was carefree. We flatmates all got on well, we had fun boyfriends, and we shared a lot of good times.

The cavalcade of early '70s fashion buzzed right outside our front door on King's Road. Androgynous hippies strolled by, the sweetish smell of cannabis wafting around their golden heads. It was shades of Golden Gate Park, except that this lot wore clothes, the fashion of the time: platform shoes with soles four inches thick peeped precariously from beneath tight, frayed denim or velvet bell-bottomed trousers; girls sported outrageous buttock-cheek-exposing hot pants in shiny silvery materials—like turkeys prepared for a Christmas roasting—or long, flowered cheesecloth skirts and no bras. Outfits were topped by small tie-dyed T-shirts, and their wearers adorned with

96

beaded necklaces, bracelets and anklets made from nuts, seeds and coloured glass. Embroidered Indian purses, stuffed with 'roll-ups' and a little money—but no make-up—were worn crossways across the chest and hung low on the hip.

At the bus stop immediately outside our apartment there was often a mixed gaggle of flashily attractive young women with more masculine-looking, dowdy females in trousers. The latter—often dressed in pinstripe suits and even the occasional necktie—were sometimes easily mistaken for men. These women were an odd mix, but all part of the social fabric then.

It was some time later that we heard about the Gateways Club, which turned out to be just around the corner from our apartment. This now legendary lesbian club—which was used for a scene in the film *The Killing of Sister George*, starring Susannah York and the inimitable Beryl Reid—was apparently well known to everyone except us! I never saw the movie and never really understood that whole scene. It was just a strand of life in the area where we lived and seemed a perfectly natural part of the general craziness.

Each evening, as I walked the short distance to my night shift at the hospital, I passed by the most talked-about shops—Kleptomania and Granny Takes a Trip—which always had fun windows to browse. Located at World's End, they nudged up against the many second-hand shops selling short rabbit-fur jackets, ostrich-feather boas and exotic turbans, as well as expensive antique emporiums, and quirky little bric-à-brac shops that were little more than a hole in the wall.

After she married Mick Jagger, posters of

Bianca Jagger with her ebony walking stick and transparent blouses enticed customers with her sultry, come-hither looks. Glam rock and multicoloured mullets ruled the day. Rhinestones sewn onto shirts and velvet dresses, and glued onto faces, were everywhere, as was an updated version of the cloche hat, so popular back in the 'Roaring Twenties'. Roxy Music, Bryan Ferry and David Bowie ruled the airwaves. This was the era of psychedelic rock (and behaviour to match!) with The Rolling Stones and Pop Art adding to the anarchic, exciting mood of the time.

Yet, coming as I did from a conservative rural background and a strict upbringing, and now a member of the disciplined and (back then) strait-laced nursing profession, I always felt something of an outsider. A bit like the little match girl, nose pressed up against the windowpane, I was an observer, always looking in but never quite belonging.

My flatmates were the same as me in this way. We had a lot of fun, but we were never part of that wild scene. The restrictions of our upbringings had shaped our behaviour and now resonated down the years, keeping our feet on the ground. But we could certainly enjoy life from the sidelines.

I spent time with a couple of US Army officers I'd known in Vietnam who were on leave in London. They couldn't believe their eyes when I walked them down the King's Road. One of them, a dental surgeon from New York with whom I had worked in Qui Nhon, embraced the whole scene rather too enthusiastically and ended up in a police cell overnight. When I picked him up the next morning he still had some tiny rhinestones stuck around his eyes, the remnants of bright-green eye-shadow on his lids, and strings of beads beneath his conservative shirt. As we left, a burly police officer, trying not to grin, handed him a magnificent pink ostrich-feather fan and a tiara, saying, 'Don't forget your property, sir.' I didn't ask!

*   *   *

Working the night shift in the emergency room at St Stephen's, I certainly saw the often terrible consequences of these hedonistic times, as drugs and alcohol wreaked havoc. The Chelsea and Westminster area housed many celebrities of the music, film, media and political worlds. Many of our famous patients were brought in regularly by experienced ambulance crews who became inured to who and what they had to deal with. Bound by confidentiality, I am unable to name names, but many were instantly recognisable.

Four months prior to my start at St Stephen's, Jimi Hendrix had been brought in, full of red wine and sleeping tablets and already dead. He had choked on his own vomit.

One morning in October 1972, not long before I left St Stephen's and just as I was preparing to go off shift at 8 a.m., I had to stay and help in our resuscitation area where a patient who'd had a severe heart attack had been rushed in. We all, doctors and nurses, fought hard to help him back to life but he was an elderly man and our efforts were in vain.

As the time of death was noted, an administrator walked in to tell us the press were gathering outside. It turned out that our patient was none other than Dr Louis Leakey, the eminent, world-famous archaeologist and anthropologist. This extraordinary man, who had shaped our understanding of human origins and who so loved the wildlife of Africa, was now gone. I walked home slowly, feeling very sad but, at the same time, silently applauding the life of this dedicated scholar and courageous man.

The paramedics and police in the Chelsea precinct became good friends of mine. Their kindness towards the 'regulars'—the elderly homeless on their patch—was touching. Knowing as they did which hospitals in the area were the busiest on a particular shift, they selected the least busy departments to present with those scooped up from the gutter. These were the unfortunate down-and-outs, overdue for a good scrubbing with soap and hot water, a change of clothes and something to eat and drink. The police, as much as the paramedics, knew the nurses in the various emergency rooms in different parts of central London would help, if they weren't too busy. At St Stephen's there was a storeroom where we kept a huge carton of clean, second-hand clothes and shoes. It was topped up regularly by the Salvation Army and kind members of the public.

I settled into the Senior Nurse position on permanent night duty with ease although, after my recent experiences in Vietnam, I was uneasy and distressed that so many people living in a peaceful and civilised country such as ours were so hell-bent on self-destruction in the supposed pursuit of having a good time.

Why were they so disillusioned, so seemingly

intent on blotting out the realities of everyday life? I was reminded of the drug-taking kids who were brought in to the hospital in Vancouver. I was just thankful to be back home, where no mortars exploded to kill or maim the citizens, no tanks patrolled menacingly on our streets, and no flames of napalm were burning our children. However, nobody in London who ever read a paper or watched the news could escape the dreadful images of war—all too familiar to me—that continued to come out of Vietnam.

* * *

On every shift, at about four in the morning, a natural lull fell upon the endless admissions of druggies, alcoholics, victims of traffic accidents and life in general, before the usual early-morning rush of cardiac patients, victims of domestic abuse and rush-hour traffic accidents began.

During this lull, the patrolling coppers from the Chelsea 'nick' just down the road often dropped in for a cup of tea and a chat. During one such interlude, a taxi drew up at the glass-fronted main entrance and a smartly dressed man ran in. He asked if he could use the toilets as he had been 'caught short' en route from Heathrow to his West End hotel. I showed him the toilets and went back to the staff room to finish my tea. A few minutes later the man hurriedly thanked me and the taxi departed. The police sergeant asked what he had wanted. I thought nothing of it and told him the man had simply needed the toilet. Immediately the atmosphere in the staff room changed, charged with tension as the officer brusquely enquired

101

whether the man had an Irish accent. I stuttered that I hadn't really noticed, so few words had been spoken.

Within a matter of minutes orders were given via radios, and a bomb-disposal unit arrived from nearby Chelsea Barracks, surrounding the department with silent efficiency. The speed of proceedings took my breath away. Helmeted men in khaki and visors approached the male toilets with mysterious-looking apparatus on long handles and cautiously opened the cubicle doors.

This alarming episode came to nothing but was an effective lesson. It was made clear to us that everyone needed to be vigilant at all times. The troubles in Northern Ireland had intensified with the tragic Bloody Sunday massacre in January 1972, and the hatreds fuelling the chances of terrorist activity in the capital were intensifying. It seemed really bizarre to me, fairly recently returned from Vietnam, that such events were happening in what should have been the safe haven of my own country.

I began to tire of the endless problems on our streets, the self-indulgent excesses wrecking people's health. And what were politicians thinking? *They* were supposed to be the ones with a vision for the future, the decision-makers.

In mid-1972 I decided it was time to head back to Kontum, in Vietnam, where Dr Patricia Smith and the hard-pressed Montagnard people were in need of the clinical skills so apparently taken for granted in the centre of London. In answer to my letter, Pat asked me to delay coming for a couple of months until, hopefully, the now deteriorating security situation in the area had been reassessed.

Though worried by her message, and concerned for the safety of her team in Kontum, the delay helped me decide to take a trip with some friends.

14

The Hippie Trail

In the early 1970s many travellers hit what had become known in the '60s as the Hippie Trail, enjoying cheap overland travel between Europe, Asia and Australia. Old but still roadworthy 'magic' buses left from central London and some three weeks later deposited passengers in New Delhi. Many did the trek in their own camper vans, and it was well known that the best place to buy an old Bedford or VW camper was to look on the notice-board inside the Australian Embassy, because Aussies and New Zealanders in their droves were taking the scenic route to Europe via India, Nepal, Pakistan and Afghanistan.

Not all these adventurous people were young hippies living an alternative lifestyle. Many were just groups of friends wanting to see the world or couples who packed their children into their vehicles and used the trip to educate and expose them to the enriching experience of other cultures and customs.

Mary, the Canadian schoolteacher, and her boyfriend Doug were keen to take this trip, as was Pete, a jovial schoolteacher from New Zealand and a good friend of ours. The decision to do it taken, we resigned our jobs, got everything in order, and took off.

Though worried by her fees
for the salon of her team in Konton, the delay
helped me decide to take a trip with some friends

*   *   *

To save time, we flew to New Delhi and began our travels from there. India in November 1972 was not just a country; it was a mind-altering kaleidoscope of life in forms I had never before seen or even imagined.

The throngs of people in the streets could not be called crowds: they were multitudes, stretching as far as the eye could see and seeming to press in on all sides. The aroma of spices competed with the odours from open sewers; the heady scent of musk vied with the smell of sweat, and mingled with the fumes that belched from buses; buses bulging with people inside and out, hanging on to the sides and clinging to the roof with the casual skill born of necessity. Vendors were everywhere, selling 'chai'—the deliciously thirst-quenching local tea—peanuts, bananas and almost intoxicatingly sweet-smelling and beautiful frangipani blossoms threaded into garlands. Men on bicycles loaded with huge bales of stuff wobbled through dense traffic, jostling with motor scooters that appeared to be carrying entire families whose little ones balanced on the petrol tank. The lumbering, protected, sacred cows wandered at will, seemingly well used to the rhythms of the city teeming around them.

The beauty was exquisite, the ugliness the worst imaginable. Beggars swarmed everywhere, among them children with misshapen limbs who slid along the ground in the dirt, gesturing for food or money. Hollow-eyed young girls with a baby perched on their skinny hips stared balefully. Old men with weeping sores sat on the pavements and gazed vacantly at the crowds. Yet, in the midst of this grinding, appalling poverty, wealth flourished behind large, elegantly wrought iron gates through which we glimpsed the manicured lawns and exotic blooms of lavish estates and maharajas' palaces. Everything we saw was, in its way, fascinating, but it wasn't always easy to accept, and Mary in particular was finding it difficult to process the more disturbing aspects.

We travelled on public transport to Lucknow and on to Varanasi (also known as Benares), the holy city on the Ganges where we witnessed more extraordinary sights to assault our senses—and our Western sensibilities. Here, on the banks of this most holy of rivers, the bodies of the dead were burned on funeral pyres; here, the people bathed and washed their clothes in the river and, at dusk, sent hundreds of tiny candles placed on leaves to float out on the water, their delicate flames flickering until they slowly disappeared—each one representing a prayer.

We went into one of the dozens of sari and fabric shops and marvelled as a cheerful salesman unrolled, with dramatic flourishes, great swatches of silks and chiffons, cottons and rayons in vivid ribbons of colours so exotic we were unable to name them.

Next, we travelled up to Nepal and Kathmandu in little buses obviously built for smaller people than us. Nonetheless, as we chugged up mountain passes and careered around hair-raising bends with sheer drops to one side, the scenery was absolutely breathtaking. Pete, Doug and I enjoyed the experience for the most part, but by the time we reached Nepal Mary had had enough. She made immediate arrangements to go home to Canada, via London, but she wasn't happy about travelling alone so Doug reluctantly left too. We were all sad at the parting of the ways, but so be it. Pete and I spent two days exploring the wonders of Kathmandu, amazed at the tiny streets full of little cafés where all sorts of food laced with marijuana and God knows what else was openly sold. There were a lot of spaced-out folk in that town. And a lot of scary monkeys in the monkey temple.

With just the two of us left, we arranged a trek to the Mount Everest Base Camp. I could hardly believe this was happening even while we were flying there in a twenty-seater Twin Otter plane. It made a white-knuckle landing at tiny Lukla in the Khumbu region which, at 9,380 feet, is considered the most dangerous airstrip in the world—a fact which, thankfully, I didn't know before we took off or I might never have gone.

At Lukla we met Jed, our Sherpa guide, and Aditi, our porter, who was a stocky young woman barely four-foot-eight in height. Deftly sorting through our backpacks, she took out what we needed and repacked our stuff into a single basket. She then swung it onto her back and anchored it by means of a leather band stretched across her forehead. Anything she deemed we wouldn't need was tagged and stored nearby. Head down, Aditi charged ahead, carrying all provisions, and even our cameras, in the basket.

Jed was a chilled-out young man who spoke good English and chatted away. He wanted to hear all about North Wales because he knew the Sherpa hero, Tenzing Norgay, had trained with Edmund Hillary on Snowdon in preparation for the successful ascent of Everest in 1953. Jed was very excited when I told him about their signatures on the ceiling at the Pen-y-Gwryd Hotel, still there for all to see to this day.

The mountain scenery was exquisite, the air crystal clear. It was the end of March, and the foothills were ablaze with colour. Rhododendron bushes were bowed down with their heavy purple blossoms. I thought of the River Glaslyn in Snowdonia, and pushed a stab of homesickness aside as we walked alongside a river of rushing white water, fed by the melting snows. Above all this towered the magnificent peaks of Ama Dablam and Everest. As we walked slowly along the narrow, well-defined rocky trail, we climbed higher and felt the air thinning. At times we had to press against the rock wall as a line of yaks sashayed down the trail, brushing past us, the deep sound of the large bells suspended from their necks resonating through the air.

We made frequent stops for the energy-giving chai, flavoured with delicious spices. As prepared by Jed in trekking conditions, however, it was heavily laced with condensed milk and the sickly sweetness initially made me feel nauseous. But I quickly realised the benefits and got used to the drink; even looked forward to it after the first few days.

I have rarely felt as fit and healthy as I did during that two-week trek. Pete, however, began to show signs of altitude sickness even though we had spent the requisite two days in the small village of Namche Bazaar, giving our bodies time to

107

acclimatize to the 11,300-foot altitude. Pete had seemed fine, passed his health check at the clinic, and was given his permit to trek to the High Himalayas. But barely a day's walk out of Namche he began experiencing waves of nausea and a worsening frontal headache. Jed asked Aditi to keep an eye on me and make camp for the night at the side of the trail while he took Pete back down to Namche to rest and re-acclimatize. Next morning Jed reappeared and said Pete would be fine but was not able to continue on to Base Camp. That was another four days away, and the elevation would rise to 17,000 feet.

I trekked on with Jed and Aditi. By now we were beginning to hit snow. The only other trekker we saw was Otto, a German in his late forties or early fifties who turned out to be a pretty amazing person. His right leg had been amputated mid-thigh, and he moved along with the aid of two lightweight, specially adapted metal crutches with small spiked 'feet' on them. One day he would overtake us, the next we would overtake him; a couple of times we shared a rest stop. He told me his leg had been amputated because of a melanoma. His ambition had always been to get up to Base Camp—and here he was, achieving his dream.

I realised I was having to make more frequent stops to catch my breath. I felt great, but the air was very thin. Soon I was taking three or four steps, then needing to stop, but I felt safe with Jed and Aditi keeping a close eye on me. Eventually, on the fourth day, we reached Base Camp on schedule. I was dead tired, but when we settled down in our sleeping bags at dusk I couldn't fall asleep. All that night I tossed and turned, my eyes wide open. While Jed and Aditi were out for the count, I felt my entire body was tingling and buzzing. Sleep was nowhere near, yet I was exhausted.

Next morning, as I surveyed the stark beauty above and below us, I felt tearful. My father used to say to us as children, if we voiced an opinion on something, 'Never forget. You are a mere blot on the landscape compared to the creations of Our Lord. A tiny blot on the landscape for a fleeting moment in time.'

That morning, sipping my steaming mug of chai and watching in fascination as my breath hung in the air like fluffy cotton wool tinged with gold by the extraordinarily beautiful sunrise, I understood what my father meant. Against the backdrop of these mountains towering above us, I was a mere blot, in a fleeting moment in time.

Man was no match for the grandeur of nature on this scale.

*   *   *

We trekked back down, picked up Pete who was feeling much better, and continued back to Lukla where we bid an affectionate farewell to Jed and Aditi. Then it was a flight back to Khatmandu and back to New Delhi, where the cacophony of sound and jumble of sights were a shocking contrast to the stark, silent magnificence we had left behind.

While in Delhi, we experienced one of the great highlights for any visitor to India, indeed, one of the great sights of the world, when we made an excursion to the beautiful and legendary Taj

Mahal at Agra.

Continuing our tour of India, in the teeming streets of Calcutta I was forcibly reminded of my father's emotional description of the real poverty that he had witnessed on his travels. In Bangalore we met the daughter of the Maharaja of Bangalore. She invited us home for afternoon tea and that is where I saw at first hand the gaping abyss between luxury and immense wealth on the one hand, and the destitute poor, living in the gutters right outside the gates of the palatial home.

*   *   *

By this time I was exhausted from the onslaught that is India and ready for an uneventful interlude in peaceful surroundings. So, our departure for Sri Lanka was both timely and welcome.

The recently named Sri Lanka—it had been Ceylon until 1972—was a very different cultural experience from India. The atmosphere was calmer, the pace of life not nearly as frantic. The countryside was beautiful, the beaches palm-fringed, soft and white. We watched the stilt fishermen at Hikkaduwa, who walk out into deeper water on stilts and fish from there. We watched the local divers who caught turtles and guided them to the beach, where they expertly, and cruelly, flipped them onto their backs and left them to die in the sun. Thankfully, such cruel practices have long been outlawed, but at that time polished turtle shells were on sale in many of the local shops.

The Sinhalese husband of a nursing sister I had worked with at St Stephen's invited us to stay at his

110

home south of Sri Lanka's largest city and then capital, Colombo. Mahela showed us around his impressively large estate surrounded by coconut palms. It was also rather run-down, but it was a while before Pete and I realised that our host was under house arrest. His passport had been taken from him and he was not allowed into the city.

This was our first real awareness that not all was right with the world in Sri Lanka. Then, as we continued our way round the island, we heard rumours that there was 'trouble' and we were warned not to travel to Trincomalee.

But everyone was kind and welcoming wherever we went. In Hatton, we spent a few days with a British planter and his wife. They taught us all about tea, from the planting of it to the picking, drying, tasting and grading, and on Sunday afternoon they took us to their 'tennis club' for afternoon tea.

This was like stumbling into a novel by Somerset Maugham or—even though we weren't in India— finding ourselves back in the days of the British Raj. There was even a rosy-faced vicar present, whose chubby wife was fascinated with our travels. We sat in large rattan chairs with fan-shaped backs and were served by uniformed waiters wearing white gloves. They poured our tea from silver teapots into delicate china cups. Three-tiered cake stands held dainty egg and watercress sandwiches, crusts off, and delicious-looking little cakes.

We were introduced to everyone. Our host, Tony, told us that the men, who sported linen jackets and Panama hats, were the only seven British planters remaining, and that before the end of the year they would all have left. There were a

111

few other Brits present—a couple of businessmen, a diplomat visiting the area from Colombo, and, like us, another guest or two of the planters.

The wives in the gathering wore filmy floral dresses, with wide-brimmed hats to protect their complexions from the heavy sun. Adorned with pearls round their necks and carrying white bags and gloves, they seemed to us more Surrey than Ceylon. And, while some of the men were off playing a game of tennis, the women spoke longingly of returning to England.

All of the company bemoaned the fact that it was the end of an era and they would soon have to leave Sri Lanka. They talked of how the plantations were being ruined by inexperienced new Sinhalese managers, but that struck me as being more sour grapes than accurate. I worried how they all, especially the women, would fare. The England they had recreated in Sri Lanka had all but disappeared back home. They were in for a shock.

There was a very strong sense that afternoon that the sun was setting on this corner of colonialism.

*   *   *

It was time to move on. With some difficulty, we found a freighter that agreed to take us to Penang. From there we hopped across to Singapore and stayed with friends of mine who lived on Orchard Road. Bliss. Clean sheets, warm showers and British and American Embassies where I could check out the situation in Vietnam.

Here Pete and I went our separate ways, as he

needed to return to New Zealand to find work. I could not have asked for a more fun, pleasant travelling companion, really a great guy. Sadly, years later I learned that he had been killed in a traffic accident in Australia.

The news from Vietnam was not good.

I was advised by the US Embassy that Pat Smith was about to be evacuated from Kontum, though she didn't yet know that. And while they said they could not prevent me travelling to Saigon, they told me I would be very ill advised to go.

Off I went to the British Embassy. They were a little more direct, telling me in so many words that I would be a fool to even attempt to go to Vietnam.

I was devastated. I walked for a while and found a small park with a bench to sit on. And it was there, surrounded by beautiful flowers, that the tears came as I again thought how politicians and their terrible decisions were killing innocent people.

I hoped and prayed that everyone in Minh Quy Hospital was safe and well; the tribespeople of the central mountains would have to take care of themselves. And all those dear little children in Qui Nhon, victims of that cruel war—what would happen to them all?

Then, burying my own bitter disappointment at the way things had turned out, I talked myself round until I saw sense.

It was not my war anymore.

Part Two

DOWN UNDER

15

Welcome to Oz

Plan B is for wimps, I thought, and so I never had one. Now, though, after my tears over Vietnam had dried, I knew it was time to come up with *something*—and fast.

I counted my meagre funds, then went to a small travel shop and asked where the money could take me. From the rather limited choices the travel clerk presented me with, I plumped for somewhere I'd never imagined I'd go.

The place was Darwin, capital of the Northern Territory of Australia, which had never been high on my list of places to visit, but a ticket to any of the major cities was way out of my reach financially. As for Australia, I figured the place was probably full of disgruntled Poms and that, judging from the accents to be heard all over Earl's Court, most of the country's younger population was in London anyway. Nonetheless, stranded in Singapore, heart-sore and disappointed, this seemed the ideal time to explore this place, the farthest point from my childhood world, to which my father had sailed quite regularly. He had loved the country and regaled us with many a tale about its landscape and its people, so I bought the ticket to Darwin and decided to make the best of this unexpected adventure.

So it was, in April 1973, that I flew nervously into Darwin; nervously, because I was skating on thin ice. I had bought a one-way ticket and was left with only a paltry thirty Australian dollars after I had exchanged the American money I'd been carrying. I comforted myself with the knowledge that good nurses were in short supply in Oz at the time, but when I was confronted by an immigration officer, I forgot about that and was quite convinced I would be deported as an undesirable drain on the local economy!

In the event, no one took the slightest bit of notice of me, other than to say a cheery, 'Welcome to Australia, mate. Enjoy your stay.'

I needed funds, and I needed them fast. Hotels were always looking for staff and I was young, energetic, determined and—God knows—had a complete grasp of the hard, unglamorous work that had to be done. Having found out that the Darwin Hotel was the best in this vibrant frontier town of some 33,000 people, I rode the airport bus into the centre and headed straight there. To my huge relief, my instincts were right: the harassed manager of the Darwin Hotel had several staff vacancies to fill in a hurry and I was hired on the spot. There was a staff annexe in the grounds where I was given a small room, and shown a communal toilet and bathroom at the end of the corridor. Basic, but I had certainly seen worse.

I started work immediately as a chambermaid, but my duties quickly expanded to waiting at tables or serving behind the bar. The bar bit I found scary. I had never seen such copious amounts of cold beer drunk, or heard such language used— and that was just the women! They called me the 'skinny little Pom', but I gave as good as I got and was quickly part of the busy routine.

118

Though the work was hard and the hours long—I worked many double shifts—the pay was decent and the laid-back, friendly Aussies were good people and fun to be around. At first their unusual, and often irreverent, turns of phrase were hard to figure out, but I cottoned on soon enough.

In the three weeks I spent in Darwin, I was unable to see much of the place because I worked such long hours. My days consisted of stripping and making up beds, cleaning bathrooms and bedrooms, corridors and public rooms, then changing my sweat-soaked uniform and serving in the bar or dining room.

It was just like home, but with much better weather—in the dry season anyway. Here there *were* only two seasons, wet and dry, and fortunately for me this was the beginning of the dry, though it was still hot and humid.

*   *   *

Although my job as a hotel employee was serving its immediate purpose admirably, I needed to get back to nursing, and the sooner the better. Shortly after my arrival, knowing how slowly the wheels of bureaucracy turned in all countries where the British had left their footprint, I filled out the requisite application forms to register as a nurse in the Northern Territory and wider Australia, and discovered that the legalities differed from state to state. This reminded me of Canada, where the system was very similar. Professional qualifications and legal registration were scrutinised, approved, or rejected quite separately in each state of the country. Coming from the small island that was the

UK, this seemed to me not only time-consuming but unnecessary. I couldn't, and still don't, understand why somebody who can legally practise as a nurse—or doctor or teacher, come to that—in one part of the country can't do so in other parts of the same country.

Many of the houses in Darwin were built on pillars, with a space left underneath to park vehicles or to use for storage. I remember thinking some of them looked as though a puff of wind would blow them down, not realising how prophetic that thought turned out to be some eighteen months later when Cyclone Tracy wrecked the place.

Guests at the hotel were a mix of international tourists, well-heeled compared to the hippies who slept out on the beaches or in the many backpacker hostels around. Most visitors to this isolated tropical area, with its gorgeous beaches and unpolluted waters, had come there after exploring India and Southeast Asia, while a number of businessmen turned up looking to develop profitable interests in this modest but rapidly growing place.

I had seen a small group of Aborigines hovering around the bus station when I arrived in town and was struck by how different their facial characteristics were in comparison to anyone I had come across before. I knew only a little about these extraordinary people, who had survived such a harsh environment for tens of thousands of years, and I looked forward to learning more. But this would have to wait: I never saw an Aborigine as a guest in the hotel, nor even just for a meal in the dining room or a drink in the hotel bar, and there were none among the staff either. I wondered why, but I instinctively sensed how these people—casually referred to as the 'abos' or the 'black fellas'—were regarded and was unpleasantly reminded of the plight of the indigenous people in Vancouver. I forced myself to keep these thoughts well in check.

Something I'd not seen anywhere else was how all men who worked in offices and banks, or other public institutions, wore smart uniforms of colour-coordinated short-sleeved shirts and shorts, with knee-high socks. It looked very strange to me, coming as I did from a country where the 'uniform' of their counterparts was a pinstripe suit and a 'stiff upper lip'. When I went to the local bank to open an account, there they all were: beige shorts, knee-length socks and sparkling white shirts with the bank's logo pinned above the breast pocket. No stiff upper lip though; the faces of the bank staff were open, tanned and jovial but, for all the friendliness and informality, the efficiency was impressive.

With no time to get out there and explore, I gleaned information about the surrounding environment from the tales told by customers at the bar. One French guest stepped on a well-camouflaged reef stonefish and had to be rushed to hospital, which is how I learned about this venomous creature that lurks among the rocks and coral in the azure tropical waters off Northern Australia.

A small group of Japanese geologists were looking at the opportunities offered by the rich deposits of various ores, gold and natural gas, yet just thirty years earlier the Japanese were the

121

enemy and had made more than sixty bombing raids on this little town, killing well over two hundred people. I often stopped to admire the beautiful opals, mined in Coober Pedy and Lightning Ridge, which were displayed in the hotel's gift shop. In the coming years I would learn more about these exquisite milk-and-fire opals.

A couple of Hungarian travellers regaled me with stories of hunting and wrestling crocodiles. I didn't believe a word they were saying until they showed me photographs of themselves thrashing about as they came to grips with one of these creatures. My God! Australia was about so much more than I had realised.

*   *   *

With a few hundred dollars in my newly opened bank account, I felt safe enough to travel further south. Since hotel staff are often on the move, and I'd told Mr Morgan the manager from the outset that I wouldn't be staying longer than a month, there was no problem about my departure. In fact, someone took my place the day I left, though I wouldn't have wanted the reputation of a local character I met at the bar whose nickname was 'five-day Charlie'. When I asked why he was called this, one of his friends said, 'It's because that is the longest he's ever held on to a job!'

Aalbert and Ingrid—who had formerly been a nurse herself—were originally from Holland. They managed a cattle station close to Alice Springs and I met them when they were staying at the hotel. When I heard they were driving back to Alice Springs I offered to help with petrol costs and share the driving in exchange for a ride, and they were happy to take me along.

In their rugged Land Rover they carried all the necessities for driving almost a thousand miles through the Australian desert: plenty of water, a compass, jerry cans of fuel and extra oil, not to mention shovels, ropes, two spare wheels, extra fan-belts, and some sacking for the wheels to grip in case we got bogged down in sand. And then, of course, there was the food and a few utensils. I learned a lot about safety on the desert tracks during that trip to Alice, driven for the most part along the Stuart Highway. As a necessary safety measure, Aalbert had informed the police of the date and time of his departure and the details of his route, and would again notify them of his safe arrival.

Very quickly after leaving Darwin, the city's lush tropical foliage gave way to a landscape dotted with scrubby little bushes. Soon, terrain became hard-packed desert, increasingly (and dramatically) red in colour due to the iron oxide deposits in the sand. I was in the famous Australian outback, an infinity of space that is difficult to describe without resorting to words such as 'vast', 'endless' or 'panoramic', none of which is quite adequate enough to capture the quality and atmosphere of this gigantic landscape. The unpaved road stretched ahead to a distant horizon, and the sun beat down mercilessly, hour after hour, from cloudless blue skies. There was not a living soul to be seen until, over halfway to Alice Springs, we saw grey wallabies lolloping along in small herds. Smaller than their red kangaroo cousins, they didn't seem quite real to me. I wondered whether they'd escaped from a nearby zoo.

When at last we drew nearer to Alice Springs, I saw bright green flocks of budgerigars and swooping grey- and pink-breasted galahs. Sulphur-crested cockatoos—white birds with bright yellow combs, or crests—perched in the ghostly white gum trees edging the dry bed of the Todd River. Aalbert told me how, ten years earlier, he had come to be hired in Amsterdam by the Australian landowner to manage his cattle station. Aalbert had a pilot's licence, a skill required for the job because a light plane had to be used to check the perimeter fencing of the station. He explained that the first time he flew over the property with the owner, it struck him that the size of the man's land alone was the size of Holland. I remembered what my Canadian cousins said when I first visited them on the prairies of Saskatchewan: 'You look out the window here and you can see clearly for three weeks.'

Huge termite hills peppered the barren land. Every few hundred miles an isolated but very welcome rest stop loomed. In those days the Ghan railway ran only from Adelaide to Alice, so the only way for most people to travel on to Darwin was by road. Between Alice and Darwin there were very few rest stops, but they were unforgettable places where amazing characters came to slake their thirst. Mighty road trains thundered along the highway, hauling supplies in their large containers. To the drivers, time was money. At Tennant Creek, one of our stops, I was told how, when the clouds of dust on the horizon heralded the approach of the trucks, the pub owners would line up six black coffees in readiness for the exhausted drivers. It took about six attempts before their shaking hands steadied sufficiently to enable them to down a decent mouthful.

These men told of how they swallowed amphetamines so as to keep awake for hours; and of how, while trying to shave time off those cross-country marathon trips, they hallucinated as they drove. One told me how he saw huge dragons on either side of the highway, just waiting to pounce. In those days, I noticed some drivers were travelling alone. They were tough characters, who must have made bundles of money, but at what cost to their health could hardly be imagined.

Ingrid and Aalbert were a great couple and taught me a lot in our conversations on that two-day journey. I ended the memorable trip with a fond—and I knew only temporary—farewell to my delightful new friends and fell into the hotel, the Stuart Arms, where they had dropped me off. Dusty, sweaty, hungry and tired (but content with life), I needed a shower, a meal and a good night's sleep.

Then it would be time for the next challenge: the Alice Springs General Hospital ...

16

A Town Like Alice

What woman in her right mind gets up at 4 a.m. to put on a formal evening dress, primp her hair and make-up, then head off with her handsome escort in tuxedo to the dry riverbed to join others for a champagne and chicken breakfast at five o'clock?

Answer: folk in Alice Springs on Bangtail Muster Day!

I think it is the light that makes Central Australia so special. At my first early-morning picnic in the creek bed, champagne glass in one hand, chicken leg in the other, I was conscious of the cool, clean morning air brushing gently across my cheeks before the sun swiftly rose. The honey-gold tones of the sunlight turned to a rosier glow within minutes as the sun became a burning globe, gliding smoothly above the horizon while giving off a blistering heat.

In Alice Springs, as indigo turns to red, the glorious light ensures that the MacDonnell mountain range that overlooks the town takes on a majestic and magical presence.

Watching the sun come up was a special sight, but then so was the whole visual experience of Alice Springs: the light, the different colours in the rocks and mountain ranges, the sunsets, the amazing night skies. The overall feeling of being in a different and special space also gave me my first glimpse into the Dreamtime, so called by the Aborigines, for whom natural features have spiritual significance. The Dreamtime refers to the myth of creation in which the Aborigines believe: a time when huge creatures rose from a flat and empty surface, took the form of various animals, birds and insects, and carved out rivers, mountains and other features of inhabited landscapes. Their beliefs linked the indigenous people closely to their sacred places, and I came to understand why they have always respected the elements of nature and felt at one with them.

*   *   *

The Alice Springs General Hospital, which housed 120 beds, was made up of a scattering of several neighbouring one-storey buildings. Narrow concrete paths threading through the dry, dusty, heat-baked ground connected the various clinical and support areas. Noisy air-conditioning units perched clumsily on the outside of every structure. A few of the eucalyptus trees known as ghost gums threw a little welcome shade here and there, and a chain-link fence defined the perimeter of the hospital grounds.

On the other side of the main dirt road was a small park where patchy green grass and shade trees provided a place for the many Aborigines who sat waiting: waiting for a family member to be seen, to be admitted or to be discharged; and perhaps just waiting for a better life to show up.

The Director of Nursing at ASG, Joy Cruickshank, was a bustling, efficient woman with a kindly face. During my initial interview with her, she took a particular interest in my work history because her youngest brother was serving in

127

Vietnam. She had more questions for me than I had for her.

The position of Head Nurse covering the busy emergency room and outpatient departments was coming up, and she offered it to me. After a tour of those departments and a chat with Diane Clarke, the incumbent head nurse, I accepted. In the meantime, until Diane left, I would join four other new nurses at the hospital the following week, and would work on the children's ward.

I was given an apartment in a building some twenty minutes' walk from work, provided for hospital personnel. It was small, but modern, brightly painted and cheerfully comfortable.

The four nurses with whom I commenced the orientation programme that day in May 1973 were Elisabeth, a midwife from Edinburgh, prim at first, but lots of fun later; Rita, an outspoken Australian theatre nurse from Sydney; Mai, a quiet, thoughtful Swede from Lulea in Lapland, who had trained in Stockholm and, surprisingly to me, was not blonde (I do recall wondering how on earth she would deal with the heat after the snows of Lapland); and lastly Elsa, a hefty German girl with a roaring laugh to match her build, who was travelling the world on a shoestring laced with cannabis.

My first surprise was that non-Brits had to swear an oath of service, either to the Queen or on a bible, to uphold and deliver good health care to all, whenever and wherever needed.

A second surprise came the following day when we were taken on a full tour of the hospital, which was organised into standard male and female medical and surgical wards. There was a large

128

paediatric unit with a colourful playroom, ante- and post-natal units and delivery suites next to the operating rooms, and the outpatient and emergency room services where I was to work in due course. Nothing unusual, then, except that it was immediately obvious that the majority of patients were Aborigines.

When being shown around the male medical ward by a senior nurse, she took us into the toilet and shower area. With an offhand toss of her head, she said, 'The black fellas are too bloody thick to piss or shit in the lavatory.' I was a bit shocked at that. I'd soon become impervious to the salty language that was often used, but I never stopped minding about some of the sentiments behind it.

Opening each of the cubicle doors, she looked for messy evidence with which to prove her point. There was just a small puddle in one of the corners. 'No worries. You lot will see it soon enough,' was her reaction.

I wondered how long it had been since she had taken the oath to uphold standards of care, and was relieved when Australian Rita bluntly suggested that she tone down her comments.

My limited understanding of the people indigenous to this central desert area was that they would surely see water as something precious and life-giving and therefore to be protected. Certainly, the Aborigines would never contaminate water with human waste, which would perhaps explain their reluctance to use Western-style toilets.

I was to learn that some of the Arrernte (or Aranda or Arunta as they're sometimes known in English), the traditional inhabitants of the central area for 40,000 years, had never been to Alice Springs, or anywhere like it. Some of the tribesmen, and women and children, flown in by the Royal Flying Doctor Service (RFDS) when injured or really sick, had never before been in a hospital with its strange sights and smells, nor seen Western beds and bed linen. They must really have thought that 'white fellas' were too bloody thick to keep their water clean!

None of this was that difficult to figure out, but was obviously beyond the reasoning of that particular nurse. Some people, I've learned, are so quick to judge, without attempting to learn about or understand the beliefs and customs of others.

*   *   *

Alice Springs was, and is, the beating heart of Central Australia—and of the outback. In 1973 the population was some 15,000 strong, spread over a wide area. Known as the Red Centre, this oasis town lies between several deserts where temperatures can vary by 28° C. In summer the average then was 37° C and in winter 7.5° C.

Thank God I arrived as winter was approaching. The month of May was still very hot during the day, but the desert nights were cold.

The dusty town was strung out for some four blocks on either side of Todd Street, the main drag. It was easy to walk around town, and this I did to get my bearings.

From the top of Anzac Hill there was a good view of the eastern and western MacDonnell ranges. Towards the east, the Todd River, bone-dry most of the time, sliced through part of the

130

town. The characteristic ghost gums lined both banks, and provided welcome shade. It was here that I saw my first wild camels.

Towards the middle of the nineteenth century, camels had been imported from Afghanistan to help in crossing the deserts to journey into the unexplored interior. Now there were many of them, roaming free. I learned that donkeys roam where camels roam, natural friends in this isolated oasis in the centre of red earth and intense heat.

The famous Ghan train, which ran only between Adelaide and Alice when I was there in 1973, was named in tribute to the Afghan camel drivers who had originally brought the beasts to help settle the outback of Australia.

It was not until the middle of the twentieth century that a significant European population came to live in Alice Springs. Aboriginal families were still walking out of the desert as late as the 1960s, many of them to have their first contact with white Australia. Through word of mouth they would be made aware that their world was slowly changing. They would hear from others that there was a town, and that the government now wanted these nomadic people to be accounted for.

So it was that I found myself in what was still a very young town, and one which, like Darwin, had the same frontier feel about it. There were, though, already the makings of a vibrant, growing multicultural community, working towards the development of an integrated, united town with the indigenous people at its core.

*   *   *

131

In the late 1800s Lutheran missionaries from Germany began arriving, settling within the area served by Alice. They founded the Hermannsburg, Finke River, Ti Tree, Papunya and Santa Teresa Missions, which provided shelter, health care and education to the desert dwellers. More sprang up over the years.

Many of the patients in the hospital had been trucked in from the missions or flown in from the more distant cattle stations but, more commonly, they came from the squalid camps strung out along parts of the Todd River bank, as well as in the dry riverbed, where I had picnicked.

My few weeks on the children's ward were a great way to meet my first Aborigines. The children were adorable. Chubby, dimpled and shy at first, they soon responded to treatment and began playing in the ward playroom. Each floor had an interpreter who spoke the most common dialects—Pitjantjatjara or Pintupi.

The most common complaints were chest infections, pneumonias, gastroenteritis, eye and ear infections or trauma—burns and broken bones. The senior paediatrician on the unit was a forward-thinking young man from Melbourne, who invited local tribal medicine men to attend ward rounds. I only ever met two of them, but I was so impressed with this bridging of knowledge: ancient medicine working hand in hand with modern practice.

The medicine men were regarded by their communities as figures of great wisdom and stature, and believed to have immense power and authority on spiritual matters. They were trained by elders from an early age and initiated into the deepest of tribal secrets. Sorcery and the casting of spells were often used.

The tribal practice for treating chest infections was to lie the patient face down, with head tipped lower than the feet, over a smoking fire to encourage coughing and 'get bad stuff out of chest'.

The young mothers or older grandmothers were always present at the hospital with their children. They sat quietly, often expressionless, but taking everything in.

All too soon it was time for me to transfer to the emergency room and outpatient department to take up the duties for which I'd been hired.

17

Emergency Room

In 1973 the hospital's 120 beds served an area of 1.6 million square kilometres (over 600,000 square miles).

The emergency room team of doctors and nurses functioned well, as did all the hospital personnel, but during the three years I nursed at Alice Springs General, it was obvious that the demands being made on the services were steadily increasing. There were plans for a larger, more modern hospital, but this would not be completed until 1978.

In the meantime, our ER department was made up of a large, central reception desk and nurses' station—where various telephones and a short-wave radio ensured rapid connection to other essential services in town—and a well-equipped, two-bedded resuscitation area occupying the space adjoining two small operating rooms. One of these ORs was for dealing with so-called 'dirty' cases such as abscesses needing to be lanced, wounds needing to be trimmed and cleaned out— 'debrided' is the medical term—messy lacerations and multiple injuries; the second room was kept clean for carrying out minor but invasive surgical procedures and treating burns. There were two treatment rooms and six curtained cubicles where patients were initially seen and assessed, and the hospital's X-ray unit was close by.

Leading from the emergency room, a second and much larger area was home to the busy outpatient department. Here, consultants in different specialities held their busy clinics in a corridor of eight rooms leading off a large waiting area. There was also a dressings clinic where old wounds were revised, assessed and re-dressed.

Diane Clarke, the outgoing Head Nurse, had been running these departments for a year, but she was now homesick and preparing to return to Melbourne. She looked tired and washed out, but managed the handover of her job to me with great efficiency, and gave me an excellent insight into what I would shortly have to cope with.

I found the high percentage of major traffic accidents occurring in the Northern Territory perplexing, given that the roads were wide and carried little traffic—and anyway, oncoming traffic was heralded for some time by the clouds of thick red dust kicked up by approaching road trains, rough-terrain four-by-fours, and the few tourist buses. How, I wondered, could vehicles travelling such long distances, with drivers able to see what was coming for miles, end up slapping into each other at high speed?

Diane explained that driving such long distances at speed and in sparse traffic can have a hypnotic effect on already fatigued drivers. Often when they saw a vehicle in the distance, unless they were extremely alert at the time, drivers found themselves mesmerised by an approaching vehicle, and a collision could easily follow. At that time there was no national blanket speed limit outside of towns. I was warned several times to 'just go bush' if driving outside of Alice and seeing a road train coming towards me. 'Just go bush' meant get the hell off the main highway and onto the scrubby red dirt at the side, giving the oncoming vehicle a wide berth.

And no wonder: the road trains, a common sight in the outback, were heavy-duty monster trucks, built to cope with harsh conditions, that could pull three or more trailers with 53-metre-long rigs. They carried—and still carry—livestock, fuel, mineral ores or general freight, and were often to be seen ploughing along the Stuart Highway between Darwin, Tennant Creek and Alice Springs. Restricted, for obvious reasons, to the outback, road trains were not to be messed with.

Alice Springs was the only place I have ever come across where a senior nurse, if she could be spared, went out on ambulance calls. In order to familiarise myself with what I might be sending any of the nursing team to cope with, I went out twice myself. Both calls were to traffic accidents, one with a fatality.

The experience left me with a deep respect for the firemen who have to cut people out of mangled wrecks, and the police, who have to figure out what happened when casualties are shocked, disoriented, drunk, or worse. The ambulance crews then were not the highly trained paramedics of today, but were inevitably often first to arrive at a ghastly, bloody, complicated scene. And, my God, minimal training or not, their calm presence as they quickly took in the carnage gave firm reassurance and comfort to the injured.

Horrifying sights are, of course, seen by doctors and nurses the world over, but by the time trauma patients are received into the emergency room, they have been scraped off the road, cut out of their smashed vehicle by others, placed on a stretcher and brought in between clean sheets. We are spared the initial mess of an accident, but my eyes were truly opened when I saw what those first on the scene have to deal with, and the vital work of firemen, police and ambulance crews left a deep and lasting impression on me.

*　　　*　　　*

The team of young nurses and doctors at Alice Springs General were from many parts of the world. At various times there were Swedes, New Zealanders—affectionately known as Kiwis—Germans, French, Dutch and Brits all working their way around Australia. Most of the Australians were from the bigger cities down south, and had come to the Territory for the outback experience. The melting pot of nationalities added spice to the mix, and the pooling of our talents and training led to stimulating debate, which could only improve our professional skills.

An essential asset to the ER team, and the hospital at large, were the young Aboriginal interpreters. Their role, as any interpreter will tell you, was never easy, as they had first to understand what a doctor or nurse wanted to convey. This in itself can be difficult. In addition, many questions that need answers, if the correct diagnosis is to be made, are of a very personal or intimate nature, and this can be embarrassing or—more seriously— taboo for a youngster to ask an elder. On top of all this, a worried, bemused or frightened patient might speak a dialect not easily understood by the interpreter. Our interpreters—Betsy, Annie, Jimmy and Johnny—between them spoke Warlpiri, Pitjantjatjara or Aranda (now spelled Arrernte), the major languages of the area, but there were many Aboriginal dialects, and communication often got lost in translation.

Retaining Aboriginal personnel was a problem. Attempting to factor into a duty rota an important cultural tradition such as the legendary 'walkabout' was just plain impossible. I would not presume to try and explain the roots of this— which may or may not have spiritual meaning—but my understanding is that it is a nomadic excursion into the bush, a temporary return to traditional life taken between periods of work. It begins with an unspoken urge to depart, without notice, for an unspecified amount of time, and to return in the same manner. I was beginning to understand why Diane had looked so tired and washed out! Anyone who has worked with tribal peoples whose

137

heritage has been disrupted will recognise the trait of 'going walkabout'. This was, and is, particularly prevalent in this part of the world, but I was to come across it again among the Inuit in the Canadian Arctic.

Delightful members of the team, our interpreters were hugely helpful in untangling the many misunderstandings that frequently arose. The clash of cultures often led to amusing incidents, but many could lead to confusion, anger and, on occasion, violence. But when Betsy wanted to go on walkabout, she went. They all did. Coming to work each day at a set time and carrying out their responsibilities efficiently and appropriately worked well for a while. But only a while. On any day, at the start of a shift I would ask where Jimmy was, hoping he'd be there. Perhaps there was a fracas in one of the cubicles between a doctor and patient, and we needed an interpreter pronto.

'Maybe him go walkabout, Sister,' one of the others would say.

'Can someone please find out where he is?' I would command my troops.

And, maybe four days later, someone would amble up and tell me, 'Yes, Sister. Jimmy go walkabout.'

'How many days will he be gone?'

'Nobody know. Him go walkabout.'

How could we run a department like this, I wondered despairingly at first. But, of course, for all the hair-tearing frustration, we somehow did. All clinical areas in the ASG had to deal with this laid-back approach to employment, and so did all the other facilities in the town that required the

138

Anne at Girl Guides (2nd left, back row) circa 1955

Newly qualified
nurse, 1962

In Italy, when I was a
nanny, 1963

Cassiar Hospital, 1967. Now all gone

Mother and children at nursing station, Eskimo Point, 1978

Anne wearing traditional Inuit amautik

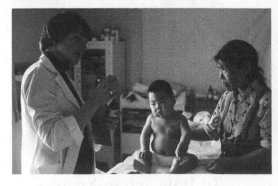

Mother and baby health check, 1978

Ready for the hunt,
wearing caribou
hide for warmth

Drying caribou
skins

Dog Sledding,
Churchill,
1978

Henry, our interpreter, with Dorothy and Jim,
Royal Canadian Mounted Police officer

Radio
station,
Eskimo
Point,
showing
Inuktituk
language

Resting
in peace,
Inuit
graves at
Eskimo
point

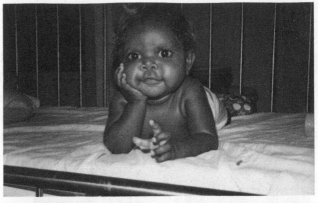

I'm ready for
my close up!

Betty, making coolomon for
carrying food or babies

Aboriginal camp elder

Joe, holding the
king brown snake

Anne and friend, up early on Bangtail Muster day for chicken and champagne breakfast

Anne in fancy dress as a 'dunger' – Bangtail Muster parade, Alice Springs, 1974

Anne and Jim, Aboriginal elder

Eskimo Point, now named Arviat, 2009

Inuit campaign to save seal hunting rights

One of the many uses for antlers

Cassiar's derelict asbestos waste pile, abandoned in 1992

Rounding up
the 'brumbies',
twenty-first
century style

Aboriginal
stockman –
how long will
the old ways
survive?

Stockman
in action

All photos this page by kind permission of Hans of Todd Photoshop,
Alice Springs

language skills of Aboriginal people. I often wanted to go walkabout myself, but my cultural work ethic was aeons of time distant from that of the desert dwellers. This was going to take time ...

A couple of months after Jimmy's disappearance, he suddenly turned up—in his uniform—ready for the start of a shift, and was upset that his job had gone to someone else. I tried to explain to him that he could be placed on an 'on call' list—which I called my 'walkabout rota'. He could come in when someone else went on walkabout. That did not work terribly well either.

This puts me in mind of Evonne Goolagong, the famous and much-loved Australian tennis champion, herself part Aborigine, who won seven Grand Slam singles titles during the 1970s and early 1980s, including two at Wimbledon. A wonderful athlete, exceptionally graceful and very quick around the court, her pace would sometimes inexplicably become erratic. Interestingly, the late legendary commentator, Dan Maskell, would say at such moments, 'Uh-oh, Evonne's going walkabout!' Today, Evonne Goolagong Cawley, as she became when she married, is an MBE, a consultant to the Indigenous Sports Programme, and raises funds for sports equipment for Aboriginal communities. She has been a great role model for her people.

*   *   *

Responsible for overseeing the health of all those who lived outside of Alice Springs proper was the RFDS—the Royal Flying Doctor Service—whose main base was a few streets away from the hospital. Dr John Hawkins was in charge during my term. A surgeon from Tasmania, this strong, quiet, unassuming man was well respected throughout the area. Several nursing sisters manned the base and flew out to cattle stations and homesteads, to Lutheran missions, and to road accidents on the highway if they were more than a couple of hundred miles from Alice.

All homesteads—as the ranch-style main dwellings on cattle or sheep stations were known—throughout the outback had two-way short-wave radios with which they could contact the base. Each homestead was given a large first-aid box, a veritable pharmacy that looked like a tin trunk, with some fifteen numbered compartments to it. Each compartment contained a treatment of some sort: several kinds of antibiotic, and a good stock of painkillers, antiseptic lotions and creams, sterile dressing and suture packs, syringes, needles, ampoules of local anaesthetic and bandages. When a call came in to base from a homestead or mission hundreds of miles away, the doctor or nurse on duty assessed the information given and diagnosed the problem where possible. The caller was then told to open the relevant compartment, where they would find instructions explaining how to use the contents.

Community health nurses attached to the RFDS visited homesteads every few months to check the contents of the first-aid boxes, and to answer any queries. The nurses always travelled in twos, never alone, and were well prepared for any emergency, exactly as my friends Aalbert and Ingrid always were. (We had kept in touch and would meet up from time to time when they came into Alice for supplies.) Most of the stations had managers, and nurses and teachers were high on the 'suitable wife' list of those single men living in the isolation of those stations.

Again, as part of my orientation to the area I was invited to visit two cattle stations by Mary, an Irish nurse who had lived in Alice for four years and loved it. She was a community health sister and good company—which was just as well because we were gone for a week, and travelled a total of 750 miles.

Mary always carried a compass but knew her way and, as we bowled along the dusty red-dirt roads to the first station we were visiting, we passed a huge sign saying: WE DON'T PROSECUTE TRESPASSERS. WE SHOOT THE BASTARDS. I just love the Aussies! Can you imagine a sign like that in Britain—the health and safety brigade would foam at the mouth!

After the signpost, we barely saw a thing, but Mary pointed out every now and then what she called her landmarks. A wattle bush, stunted and struggling, was her first one.

'What?!' I yelled. 'You call that a landmark?'

'OK . . . How many other wattles can you see?' came the reply.

The land was indeed as flat as a pancake—no wattle, no anything.

The next landmark was a little pile of beer cans and small rocks, built up like a drunken cairn. I ask you!

I sure hoped her compass was working efficiently. This did not look like a good place to get lost. Eventually we arrived at an untidy scattering of barnlike outbuildings. A water-pump

141

windmill stood tall and proud, its metal blades moving listlessly in the evening breeze.

A beautiful flame tree threw shade over part of the large wooden homestead, which had a verandah of weathered planking running around it. Some overstuffed chairs, bursting at the seams but comfy just the same, sat next to a couple of small tables with pretty lace cloths on them. A bowl of crisps sat on each table with some cans of beer and an Esky—the ubiquitous icebox that everyone has in the outback—close to one of the chairs, where more precious cans of beer sat packed in ice.

Mary shouted a cheery 'Hello, here we are', and Françoise, the new wife of Jim Hilton, the manager, ran out to greet us.

Françoise was French. She had been a teacher in Lille, went to Australia to teach French at a high school in Sydney, and met Jim, a tough Aussie farmer. This unlikely couple married, and he carried her off to his isolated cattle station.

We had a marvellous evening meal, a hearty stew that had been made to satisfy Jim; for us, however, Françoise served a separate dish of the same stew but enhanced for our benefit with delicate French herbs. Jim had no time for 'that darn fancy stuff' so Françoise went slightly nuts in the kitchen whenever she had guests. That explained the pretty lace tablecloths, so at odds with the serious beer-drinking to come!

We stayed overnight and all of the next day, before travelling on to the next homestead. Mary knew the ropes, and slung our small bags onto the bunks in one of the outbuildings where we were to sleep.

We each had flashlights to use in the night if a trip to the 'dunny' (the loo) was needed. The flashlights were necessary because the loo was a few hundred yards from where we were sleeping. At about 4 a.m. I woke up, needing to get rid of some of the beer drunk the previous evening. I put on my desert boots and walked carefully towards the toilet shed. The night was cool and clear. Next to the toilet was a bucket of water with which to flush; another bucket of water was for washing hands at the tiny sink, next to which was a small, embroidered towel (that would be a Françoise touch), hanging from a nail (that would be Jim).

Holding the flashlight in my mouth, I began raising the bucket of water to flush the toilet and noticed a piece of rope over the side of the bucket, half in the water, half out. Suddenly the rope moved, and I realised with horror that I was looking at a snake. I screamed, dropped the bucket and the flashlight on the floor, and fled. I was met by two of the Aboriginal stockmen and Mary, running to see what the screaming was. The stockmen sped into the dunny, we heard some scuffling and swearing, then one of them came out holding a long, fat snake.

I'm not the fainting type, but I nearly keeled over when I saw that creature. The guy with the snake, clearly amused, said, 'No worries, Sister. This feller won't hurt you. Carpet python, see? He won't hurt anybody,' and he held the snake's head against his dimpled cheek, while he and his mate had a good laugh.

By this time Jim had appeared, with a very strong flashlight. God in heaven, was every visit to the toilet going to be like this?

143

They all thought it was hilarious, but I didn't sleep another bloody wink that night, and swore that I'd never again drink after 6 p.m. Well ... I meant it at the time.

Next day Mary showed me the first-aid equipment and explained how to check the register of accidents and minor illnesses against the record of treatments given and medication used.

I was seeing the fruits of the dedication and ingenuity of Reverend John Flynn who, back in 1928, saw the need for emergency and preventative health care in the isolated communities of the Australian interior. Thanks to his vision, the now legendary Royal Flying Doctor Service—which Reverend Flynn called 'a mantle of safety'—was born. The base at Alice Springs was opened in 1939.

Françoise was nervous about some of the points Mary was raising, like maybe having to suture lacerations, so Jim disappeared to the huge larder at the back of the kitchen area, returned with a huge slab of beef, and threw it down on the large wooden kitchen table. He reached for one of the sharp knives next to the stove, slashed the beef and said, 'There. Stitch that up, Fran,' and walked out roaring his head off.

I spent an hour showing Françoise how not to be scared of a laceration and how to suture it up. We made several slashes into the glistening hunk of prime beef before she overcame her nervousness, and was soon adept and confident in her handiwork.

While that was going on, Mary was over in the 'school room', another building, where eight children, a mix of white and Aboriginal six- to ten-year-olds, were sitting around a short-wave radio speaking in turn to their teacher at the School of the Air in Alice Springs. A student teacher up for a couple of weeks to see how it all worked was overseeing the kids, but usually Françoise was in charge. Not for the first (or last) time, I marvelled at the ingenuity of this country, and understood even more clearly what a catch a nurse or teacher was for a station manager on the hunt for a wife.

The little Aborigines were the children of the stockmen and other personnel at the station. I was becoming aware of the kinship, warmth and efficient organization that, despite the awesome isolation, linked all these amazing people populating the Red Centre.

Aboriginal stockmen were in great demand. Their horsemanship skills were second to none. Later I was to witness some of them breaking in 'brumbies' at Ross River Station, closer to Alice than Françoise and Jim's station. Brumbies are the wild horses that have inhabited, and thrived, in vast areas of the Australian outback ever since they were turned loose after the great Australian Gold Rush in the mid-1850s. These feral horses would be the equivalent of the mustang horses in America.

Australia has a huge population of these tough creatures and at times they have to be culled. Their ability to dig deep holes to find water is proof of their learned behaviour. Their strength and endurance was used in races, which I was to see later in my stay.

The stockmen were as one with these horses. It was a beautiful sight witnessing the affinity between the human and animal desert-dwellers.

145

I learned such a lot on that trip. When I was back in the emergency room in Alice, I could now envisage the folk who called for help and advice to the RFDS base up the road; and if anyone from the base had to fly out to a station emergency, they would tell us so that we would be ready to receive them at the hospital.

Like emergency rooms the world over, we were always on stand-by for any emergency at the airport. Several times a year there would be a call placing us on alert status. Often it was 'engine problems, emergency landing anticipated'.

Fortunately nothing serious happened in my time at Alice, but one day a young locum doctor with a great sense of fun was up from Adelaide for a few weeks. He answered the 'red phone'—the airport alert telephone. He was nearest and picked it up without thinking. Replacing the receiver he turned to me and, totally deadpan, said, 'Stand by for emergency landing, Sister. Undercarriage problems. Shall I call the gynaecologists, or will you?'

18

Love and Stuff

One of the first items on the 'to do' list when arriving in a different part of the world from your own natural habitat, is to suss out sources of entertainment, relaxation—or even romance— while discovering what makes a place tick.

I love any medium that honours and celebrates

146

local history, so in Alice Springs that meant checking out the local folk club. I was not disappointed. The place was well attended and flourishing: once a week earnest, bearded young men would play everything from fiddles, banjos and penny whistles, to washboards, a tea chest and mouth-organs; some of them, lacking a more recognizable instrument, even slapped pairs of spoons on their thighs—clad in the flared, patchworked trousers of the 1970s. Sometimes a pretty girl, headband fastening her flowing hair, coaxed a rhythm from her tambourine with a subtle shivering motion of her entire body as she sang hauntingly beside one of the bands. At the folk club, haunting ballads and convict songs rang out with soulful energy, and the audience joined in enthusiastically.

Folk songs in Australia (as in America) were a way of recording events and feelings among those who often could neither read nor write. Convicts had sung of long sea voyages—'Bound for South Australia' or 'Van Diemen's Land', and of the dark-eyed lovelies they had left behind in Cornwall, Skye or Cork. They sang rousingly of 'Maggie May', and sadly of 'The Girls of the Shamrock', passing on in time-honoured tradition the oral history of those transported to this new, exciting land to which they had been banished, often perhaps for no greater crime than stealing a crust of bread for their starving families.

Listening to these songs was a painful reminder of how harshly unforgiving the British legal system had been towards the poorest in society, and how the government of the day's ruthless plan to colonize a white Australia served as an excuse to empty the overcrowded prisons and workhouses of the eighteenth and nineteenth centuries—and later, to ship out the surplus of orphaned, illegitimate or abandoned children who were filling the grim 'care' homes of post-war Britain. Some of those babies and toddlers were loved and wanted, but their hard-pressed mothers were forced to place their children into temporary care. Despite this, some of them were caught up in the forced exodus.

As time moved on, escaped convicts became outlaws (known as bushrangers), and many of them, most famously Ned Kelly, eluded the police and turned into folk heroes. Songs such as 'The Death of Ned Kelly', 'The Wild Colonial Boy' and 'Wild Rover No More' were eventually overtaken by songs about the lives and loves of drovers and shearers: 'Click Go the Shears', 'Wallaby Stew' and 'Waltzing Matilda' were strong favourites and, listening to these songs, I was very conscious of the recent history of this vast, but still sparsely populated land.

I was also vividly reminded on one occasion down at the club, during a particularly energetic, communal rendering of 'Waltzing Matilda', of an incident in Vietnam three years earlier. I was in Kontum at the time, and one evening I witnessed a fist fight between a group of American and Australian Special Forces men. It happened during a show put on by a third-rate Australian rock group, plus an unfunny comedian, who suddenly began singing obscene words to 'Waltzing Matilda'. This provoked a verbal attack from both Australians and Americans in the audience. Given the abnormal tensions and horrors of war, flashpoints triggering fights were never far away and helped let off steam.

On this occasion, though, the comedian's dirty mouth was the flashpoint, especially for the Australians, to whom the comedian's language was a real betrayal, tantamount to desecrating the national anthem. The mayhem was stopped by several shots fired over their heads by a senior officer, but not before the hapless comic had been thrown out by the seat of his pants.

Everyone shook hands, straightened up the chairs and the show went on.

*   *   *

I don't remember ever seeing an Aborigine sitting in the audience at the folk club, or playing in any of the bands—not in 1970s Alice. The indigenous people had lived harmoniously with the land for at least 50,000 years. What stories they could surely have told, yet none were part of that scene in Alice Springs back then. Black fellas and white fellas apparently inhabited two different universes.

While tapping my toes to a lively jig one evening, I was lightly pondering these questions when I noticed a handsome man smiling at me from across the room. Eventually, and in the time-honoured way of studied nonchalance that men adopt when they spot their next conquest across a smoky room, he strolled over, cold beer in hand, drew up a chair and sat down.

'Hi, I'm Matt. Are you new in town?'

So began my three-year romantic adventure with Matt, a tall Texan computer programmer from the isolated Joint Defence Space Research

Facility (JDSRF) at Pine Gap some fifteen miles outside Alice Springs.

This was a 'secret' base that everyone seemed to know about. Several hundred American personnel worked there, with a small number of Australians alongside. Rumours abounded that the CIA and NASA were running a secret communications base deep underground, but no one I knew was remotely interested, only vaguely suggesting that it was something to do with the DEW Line.

The Distant Early Warning, or DEW, was an imaginary line drawn between radar stations. I'd heard about the DEW Line in Alaska and Northern Canada when I was in the Canadian north in the 1960s, and assumed it was something to do with warnings of activity from Russia in the days of Cold War paranoia. Similarly, I guessed the Australian DEW Line was probably part of the games that politicians play but, still bruised from my experiences in Vietnam, I was not in the least interested.

Those Americans on married contracts lived in town with their families. Single-status employees were provided with bachelor accommodation out at the affectionately known 'space base', strictly off limits to visitors. The cheerful, magnanimous American community brought the flavour of the US with them, and I was soon enjoying celebrations for the Fourth of July, Thanksgiving and Hallowe'en, and learning the finer points of baseball and basketball.

With his shock of dark hair, open face, ruggedly handsome looks and love of the great outdoors, Matt was the first man who had even come close to challenging that special place in my heart still

150

occupied by Mike, the doctor with whom I fell in love in Vietnam. The attraction between us was mutual and immediate. I was taken completely unawares by the feelings that swept over me, and the relationship quickly progressed. Over the following three years we explored Central Australia together. Life was good, and the loving was easy.

*   *   *

Matt loved dirt-bike riding, and owned a 250 Suzuki. Most weekends, sometimes with a few friends but more often alone, we took off to the surrounding canyons, gorges, rock pools and dry riverbeds of the spectacular Red Centre. Camping out for a weekend was a much easier affair than embracing the great outdoors back in Britain. No tents required, or bulky sweaters; no heavy-weather gear or primus stove. Simple basics were all you needed.

The sense of freedom was intoxicating, and we just took off, me riding pillion, with a couple of sleeping bags, a supply of VB (Victoria Bitter) 'tinnies' cocooned in ice cubes and safely embedded within a small Esky, along with a few good steaks, some snags—as the Aussies called sausages—and a small metal rack to throw over the campfire. We also cooked cobs of corn, inside their protective husks, and baking potatoes wrapped in foil, in the coals of the fire. A jerry can of extra fuel and loaded cameras and off we went. All this stuff was packed neatly onto the back of the bike, nestling reassuringly into the small of my back as we zoomed off into the great unknown.

Such trips were inadvisable during the scorching heat of the summer months, between November and February, but the rest of the year was perfect, and Matt had it down to a fine art.

Lying back on our sleeping bags and looking up at the night sky was always an unforgettable experience—but the first time I did it, tears slid down my cheeks from the sheer sense of awe at what I was seeing. The Southern Cross, or Crux, is a magnificent sight to anyone familiar only with the night skies of the northern hemisphere. The glittering night sky as seen from the outback, far from city lights and pollution, is like a milky carpet made up of billions of stars. I used to think it must be God's playground, where the Cross took on the shape of a celestial kite, shimmering high above. The beauty of the heavens, seen through binoculars in the space and silence of the night, was almost blinding.

Once again, I felt like the 'blot on the landscape' my father had so often described us as.

When these excursions first began, it never occurred to me to worry about snakes or creepy-crawlies. But the longer you spend in the outback, the more you learn about venomous king brown snakes, toxic redback spiders, and the harmless but scary-looking huntsman spiders—and the fact that we had a fridge in the hospital ER stocked with anti-venom ampoules was hardly reassuring.

Someone told us that we should carry a length of thick rope with us on these trips to the bush. This should be laid around the bedding in a wide loop, we were told, because no snakes, lizards or spiders would cross the rope. So, that is what we did, and I slept the better for it, though we always kept the campfire stoked with wood—just in case. It might have been hogwash, but I felt safer with that rope around us like a magic protective ring.

Rock pools were few and far between in the Red Centre, but when you did find one, it was sheer bliss.

One day, we swam across a small but deep pool and sunned ourselves on a flat rock in the middle of the water. Above us towered the sheer cliff face on either side of the narrow chasm in the rock. After a couple of hours, Matt swam back to land. A water snake trailed just behind him. Its head poked straight out of the water, like a sinister periscope. I almost fainted with shock. That snake swam around and around between the rock where I was, and where I had to swim to.

Easy! I would simply stay on that rock forever. No way was I going to brush up against a snake while swimming some fifty yards to shore. Matt would just have to tell the hospital what had happened to me ...

He threw pebbles at the snake, trying to drive it away without success. It was a good two hours later before he finally talked me into the swim. I was terrified, and almost ran across the surface of the dark pool to reach the safety of land. The thin, black snake didn't seem at all interested in me, but we left him still there, swimming around, proudly surveying his kingdom.

Together, Matt and I also became amateur rock hounds, scavenging around and finding ruby-red garnets of all sizes; finding zircon made me scream with excitement at first—I thought I had discovered diamonds. If only ... On the rare occasions that it had rained I learned that early morning as the sun was rising was the best time to find amethysts. Many were gem quality, and after they had been washed by rain, if you lay on your tummy and watched carefully as the sun came up, you saw them glinting in the ground.

One cool July day as we prepared to head out on the Ross River Road, we called in to the last little shop at the quaintly named Heavitree Gap for some provisions. Walking in, I was astonished to see the place decorated for Christmas. There was a large artificial tree, complete with cheerful baubles and a pile of wrapped gifts on display at its base, and the shelves were stocked with festive crackers, cakes and other Christmassy accessories. It was explained to me that, since it was as hot as hell and quite intolerable in December, some residents of Alice celebrated Christmas in July— the coolest time of year.

Makes sense in the outback, I suppose . . .

These trips were absolutely fascinating, such fun and very relaxing. There was so much to see, discover and experience, and Matt and I often talked of whether we could see ourselves settling in this amazing land.

But when it comes right down to thinking along those lines, you begin to focus on the distance from home. Homesickness is never too far away, and I had not left home with the intention of leaving permanently; I had only ever wished to seek knowledge of the world outside my island home, in the great tradition of islanders who have felt the need to explore. Australia is a very long way from Europe, and a long way from the States, and despite the carefree days and magical

154

times, it was slowly beginning to dawn on me that all was not well in paradise.

19

Dreamtime Nightmares

Working in a hospital, wherever in the world it may be, tells you a lot about a town and the people who give it colour, pace and heart. It's where you are able to take the pulse of a community.

In Vancouver, there was the distinct movement of people arriving from Asia and Europe, determined to settle and create a newer, shinier version of their old world, with the indigenous people having to fit in and catch up, or not; Cassiar revolved around the mining of asbestos, its population young, lusty and driven to working hard in difficult conditions in order to save up enough money to distance themselves from the tired old political upheavals of Europe.

Here in this desert frontier town, the spirit of the pioneering early white settlers and their courage in facing the harshness of the environment was still tangible. Their jovial, laid-back humour could not hide their determination to get the best out of this harsh, unyielding part of the continent. Cursing the heat, the 'wet', the flies and the dust—by God, Alice Springs was up and running. But again, there were echoes of indigenous people having to either change their ways or get out of the way of white man's progress.

Judging by everyone I knew, from people I met

155

socially, to the colleagues I worked alongside and the tourists in their matching T-shirts visiting for just a few days, almost everyone in Alice appeared to be passing through on their way to somewhere else.

Yet the people who had inhabited Australia for millennia and were so much a part of this fascinating landscape, called none of the shots, wrote none of the rules, guidelines or laws.

Perched uncomfortably on the periphery of this encroaching white man's world, the Aborigines were struggling to come to terms with their rapidly changing horizons. Where now was their long, proud heritage?

Those who squatted in squalid shanties around the Todd riverbed looked like a lost tribe, buffeted along by alcohol and social exclusion, with only welfare cheques to help keep body and soul together.

Those living out on cattle stations and missions were much better protected. They had work, and with it dignity, and were provided with some education for their children and at least a sense that they could belong, with folk who cared about them.

Successive paternalistic governments *did* provide a measure of health and social care countrywide for Aboriginal peoples: hospitals, visiting community health nurses and social workers were there if they got sick or injured, or were confused by the system; the little ones were vaccinated against childhood illnesses, and weighed and measured regularly to make sure their development kept up with textbook graphs and nutritional percentiles. The system took care of any visible deficiencies, but much deeper hurts were inflicted on these people, wounding spirit, pride and dignity, and this issue was not being addressed in 1970s Australia.

I undertook a four-week-long community health nurse course and became—temporarily—one of those nurses who visited the camps. Dressed in smart white uniforms, we carried small cases containing a set of scales for weighing the babies and toddlers. Amid the detritus we encountered, it was often difficult to find a clear, flat space on which to balance the scales. The large glass flagons—which held the popular, widely sold, cheap red wine that wreaked so much havoc on the mental and physical health of these poverty-stricken and aimless camp dwellers—lay empty and forlorn, alongside old mattresses with the stuffing bursting from various gashes. The remains of kangaroo carcasses, cooked on campfires the evening before and now picked clean, were tossed aside for the flies and mangy dogs to enjoy. Almost everyone asked constantly for paracetamol tablets to relieve splitting headaches that followed the drunken evenings, and we handed them out like packets of sweets. Today, I wonder at how we possibly could have thought that paracetamol would help blot out the pain these people were feeling.

Before entering the camp, one always waited to be approached and invited in by an elder. Despite the anarchic mood that often prevailed as a companion to the hangovers, I never felt anxious or afraid. The people knew us from the hospital and 'sisters' were seen as friends, always welcome. Liaising with the elders, I saw how steadfastly they

157

tried to cling to the ancient threads holding their crumbling culture together. But they would have known that times were changing.

I was reminded once again of the indigenous people living in their villages outside Cassiar in remote Northern Canada; similarly, in years to come, when visiting an African village in rural Sudan, we waited quietly in our vehicle a few yards away until the village elder signalled recognition and welcomed us in. Much later, when nursing in Saudi Arabia in the 1990s, I saw the same practice among the Bedouins in the southern deserts of the country. I came to recognize how the modern world was gradually eroding values that had survived through the ages, echoing more straightforward times free of hidden agendas.

But despite the modern assault on their customs, the elders proudly adhered then—and do now—to the rules of survival and politeness. The civilities are there to be found for those prepared to look, but how disrespectful and insensitive most of us are in our greedy, headlong rush to live *off* the land, instead of learning to live *with* it. Maybe that is the fundamental difference between the indigenous people of a continent, and those of us who like to consider ourselves so much more civilized and therefore think we know best how to live.

We look at what the land has to offer us: what is worth taking, and how we can profit from it. The indigenous peoples across continents, however, are part of their land; they have evolved over aeons, learning how to live alongside nature and survive, whether in burning deserts, frozen tundra or tropical rainforest. Always respecting plant, bird and animal life, never deliberately desecrating it, never contaminating water, knowing how precious and life-giving it is, always taking only what is required for life.

As I grew to know the Aboriginal people better, and to love the land in which I found myself, my thoughts often returned to the indigenous Montagnard tribesmen in the highlands of Southeast Asia. I met these people when I was nursing at Kontum in Vietnam from 1969 to 1970, and it was they who first taught me the true meaning of 'communism', or communal living. When the men had successfully been out hunting, the entire village shared the kill, so nobody went without food. There was no need for orphanages or care homes; motherless children were cared for by all the women, the elderly or infirm cared for by their families. Each and every person in the Montagnard community was loved and supported by the others.

These thoughts led me then—and lead me still—to wonder how and why our world has gone so wrong. Even in the small, Welsh village where I was raised during the 1940s and '50s—despite a family trauma that could forever have cast a dark shadow over my brothers and sisters—the quiet support of the villagers kept us on the straight and narrow, and has remained a stable influence in our lives. This, surely, is the way things should be. The indigenous people struggling to survive right now would agree, I know that.

So, as we press blindly on with our materialistic, acquisitive lives, barely knowing the names of our neighbours, it's surely time for us all to take stock, to rethink where we are headed.

159

One day, while I was on a routine visit to the creek bed, William, the elder of the community, welcomed me into the circle.

I sat cross-legged at the campfire, trying to ignore the drunken snoring of Brassy, Susan and the others slumped nearby. It was eleven o'clock on a Wednesday morning, and six of us were having a talk while drinking from chipped mugs of tea. The ever-present billycan simmered gently on the fire, ready to provide us with more of the stewed, but nonetheless refreshing, beverage.

Just as we were discussing some serious concerns, Joe staggered up, eyes bulging.

Now Joe, aged about thirty—it was difficult to tell, and no one knew for sure—was well known to all of us. He was diabetic, epileptic, a heavy drinker, and with a disconcertingly bad squint in one eye so you didn't know quite who or what he was looking at. Otherwise, Joe was just fine!

That morning, when Joe lumbered up, he produced a shotgun from under his loose orange shirt, aimed it right at our circle, and yelled loudly, 'Sister, Sister, get down!'

We all hit the dirt, and I do mean hit the dirt!

The sound of the shotgun reverberated loudly through the ghost gums all around us. Brassy sat bolt upright, blinked and yelled 'puckin' hell', then immediately sank, with a grunt, back into his comatose state. Quickly checking that no one was actually hurt, despite ten years having been frightened off our natural lives, I realised Joe was scrabbling around with something on the ground

160

right behind me. Slowly, he stood up, triumphantly holding aloft the long, battered remnants of a king brown snake. He had seen it slithering up behind us, had taken aim and, miraculously, killed said snake and no one else.

I jumped up and—yes, I admit it—I hugged Joe.

The police were called by a concerned bystander who witnessed the incident, in order for the presence of the gun to be registered. The police confirmed that the gun was the legal property of one of the group, but it was inadvisable for someone as unwell as Joe to have access to a firearm. I never saw a weapon in any of the squatter camps before or after that incident. The cops thanked a beaming Joe for his quick action, but made it clear that he was not to touch a gun again.

He was found dead in the camp a few weeks later, having choked on his vomit overnight.

A bit like Jimi Hendrix.

Only difference was, no one wrote about Joe's death. He was just an unknown drunken black fella.

*　　　*　　　*

The Aborigines had difficulty pronouncing the letter F. It always came out as a P sound, so, the popular flagons of wine were known as 'plagons', or, more accurately, 'them puckin' plagons, Sister'.

In emergency rooms of hospitals the world over, the human detritus washing up on a Friday and Saturday night—in the grip of alcohol and drugs, and often on the lower rungs of society—are struggling to blot out the pain of trying to 'make

161

it'. We had our share of the same thing in Alice Springs.

As I and others regularly gauged the clinical damage of stab wounds, the 'walking into a fist, a cupboard or a door' syndrome of those cursed with domestic violence, or the bloody end result of a road traffic accident, I so often heard the words, 'It was a puckin' plagon, Sister, that did it.'

Hard not to laugh, but harder still not to cry.

One busy afternoon, I heard raised voices coming from one of the curtained cubicles. It was summer, hotter than hell, and tempers were short. I went to see what the problem was.

The newly qualified doctor, who was in the middle of his eight weeks of 'outback experience', was red-faced and angry. The object of his frustration was an elder who had been flown in by the RFDS from Arltunga just a couple of days before. I recognised the man immediately: with his grey beard, red bandanna around his silvery head of thick hair, and leaning heavily on his stick carved from mulga wood, Henry cut a timeless figure, teetering with dignity between yesteryear and today.

Right now, despite the wisdom gleaned over his many years spent in the desert, he was looking perplexedly at the blond white man, young enough to be his grandson. Was he yelling loudly at Henry, or was he really railing at this incomprehensible world, so far removed from his comfort zone in Sydney, I wondered?

The nervous young interpreter, Betty, was caught in the crossfire, attempting to keep the medic happy and calm, while deeply respectful of the venerable white-haired old gentleman in front of her. Not for the first time I saw new professionalism and ancient wisdom clashing, each trying to figure out the other.

'What's the problem here?' I asked.

'This guy was here two days ago. Look at his leg, it's a bloody mess. I debrided it, dressed it and gave him a five-day course of cloxacillin. Now he's back asking for more pills because he finished the whole bloody lot we gave him in twenty-four hours. Stupid coon.'

Betty looked pained and tried to make like she was somewhere else. For her respected elder to be spoken to, or about, in such a manner was unheard of and distressing. And she was expected to interpret the words being spoken.

I knew from the expression in her eyes that she would not return for her shift tomorrow, and I didn't blame her. Great timing for a walkabout.

'What did the instructions say on his bottle?' I asked.

'Two capsules to be taken at eight a.m., twelve noon, six p.m. and ten p.m. with plenty of water,' replied the doctor.

'I don't see a wristwatch on him,' I replied, a tad sarcastically. 'Could you not have said take two capsules when the sun comes up, two at noon when the sun is directly overhead and two when the sun begins to sink in the west, the remaining two when darkness comes? Do that for five days.'

I did not learn that at school in North Wales, but it seemed obvious to my lateral-thinking brain.

'For fuck's sake, Sister. I can't think of every bloody thing.'

I pitied him. It's called a meeting of minds and takes time, kindness and the will to understand.

163

*   *   *

One day, Charlie, a strapping nineteen-year-old male, was brought to the hospital, lying prone in the back of a pick-up truck. He was carried into the ER by four friends. They came from Pupanya, one of the many far-flung mission stations that gave a name to an area of the vast outback spaces, and they seemed uneasy and reluctant to tell us what the problem was. Within minutes of bringing in their friend, they piled back into their pick-up and disappeared in a cloud of dust, but not before I recognized the fear in their eyes.

Though Charlie's eyes were open, they looked vacant. The lights were on, but no one was home. There was no response to questions, gentle prodding, or the gradually escalating painful stimuli attempted to elicit a response. He was admitted to the male medical ward but there was never a clear diagnosis and, no matter what the doctors tried, Charlie died some two weeks later. He just faded away, never speaking, eating or drinking. He had no obvious or visible signs or symptoms of disease or injury, and X-rays showed nothing.

Eventually the police discovered that he had upset someone out at Pupanya and the tribal medicine man had 'pointed the bone'. This was part of the sorcery and casting of spells practised by the Arrernte at that time. This was the only time I witnessed such a 'spell'. In fact, this was a ritual execution. The bone that was pointed at the condemned person could be human, kangaroo or emu. In Australian law, at that time, this was not

164

seen as murder.

It became clear that the young man had died of fear. There was no scientifically based medical diagnosis or clinical explanation for the fading away. Charlie believed deeply in the powers of the medicine man, and when the bone was pointed and the spell cast, his belief was sufficient to shut down his life.

Simple as that. It leaves no trace.

The power of suggestion is indeed strong.

*　　　*　　　*

One day, Brassy, my old acquaintance from the Todd River camp, was brought into the ER. Semi-comatose, stinking of alcohol, campfires and lack of hygiene due to the scarcity of water, he was carried out back to the dressings clinic.

A few minutes later, I heard a loud oath and the sounds of a disturbance coming from the dressings area. I hurried over and found the nurse assigned to deal with Brassy staring in sheer horror at his head. Trying to make him more comfortable, she had removed his bush hat, only to reveal a mass of writhing maggots covering his entire scalp. As a preliminary measure to alleviate the situation, and to give myself time to think, I quickly banged his distinctive hat back on his head.

In the ER cubicles, Bruce, one of the visiting medical students up from Melbourne, and a bit of a smart-arse, was forever moaning about how bored he was in Alice. Well, since he obviously needed to be less bored, I asked him to examine Brassy and tell me what his diagnosis was. Within seconds he returned to the front desk, green around the gills, his boredom forgotten!

I equipped Bruce with a disposable apron and gloves for protection, and showed him how to place Brassy's head over a large bowl; then how to pour a steady stream of warm, weakened solution of hydrogen peroxide all over the man's scalp, all the while gently explaining every step of the procedure to the unfortunate Brassy. As the peroxide foamed and bubbled, his head was quickly and easily rid of the wildlife. Once removed, it was clear that the scalp had been picked clean by said maggots. It seems that Brassy had fallen into the remains of a campfire quite some time earlier, probably gashing his head on the large stones surrounding the fire. Oblivious to his injuries, he had just kept his bush hat firmly clamped on to his head, leaving the maggots to do their work undisturbed: they had eaten away all the damaged, dead tissue, down to the bone of the skull, and the entire area was as clean as a whistle.

Maggot therapy has been known for centuries and is beginning to make a comeback in modern medicine. Maggots are the larvae of the blowfly and, before the advent of well-equipped field hospitals, and sophisticated transport to get them there quickly, wounded soldiers in battle zones were particularly susceptible to maggots. Strangely, but interestingly, wounds thus colonised by maggots were found to have better outcomes than those that were not—after thorough debridement and cleansing, bacteria were killed and the rate of healing was speeded up.

Bored Bruce from Melbourne certainly learned more than he bargained for the day Brassy came in!

166

The three-and-a-half years I spent in Alice Springs passed in a colourful kaleidoscope of work and play. But events at Christmas 1974 shocked everyone.

Warnings of an approaching tropical cyclone, the now famous Cyclone Tracy, were lost in Christmas Eve festivities. In the early hours of Christmas Day, with most people in their beds, Tracy struck, causing widespread damage to the town of Darwin, where my Australian odyssey had begun. Loosely designed buildings were too flimsy to withstand the force of winds that blew in at 217 kilometres (135 miles) an hour—the speed recorded at the airport before equipment was shattered.

Many communication links failed, as happens in such an event, and it was only some hours later that the full extent of the damage became clear. Rumours flew, but no one was yet sure what had occurred a thousand miles 'up the track'. A ham radio enthusiast in Alice Springs picked up signals coming in from Darwin, and so began the full realisation of the catastrophe. At the hospital in Alice, we were told that 'part of the hospital in Darwin had collapsed with loss of life'. Our Major Incident plan was put into operation, ready to receive the casualties, or refugees, expected over the coming forty-eight hours or so.

The government quickly mobilised planes to carry medical supplies and personnel, as well as sending a military team to assess the extent of the damage. A plane called in to Alice to take six

167

medical and nursing personnel up to the hospital in Darwin, and I was one of them.

We looked down as the plane circled Darwin, and I could scarcely believe what I was seeing. My first thought was that a bomb had dropped, and I tried not to think about sights I had witnessed in Vietnam.

It is always incredible to me just how resilient human beings are at such a time. Teams of volunteers had quickly cleared debris from the airport runways; men of all ages, stripped to the waist, were clearing roads and helping stunned victims of the cyclone to climb out of the debris.

The situation at the hospital, however, was nowhere near as bad as we had feared. Despite 70 per cent of Darwin's homes being destroyed in the cyclone, somehow only seventy-one people were killed. Very sadly, a large tree had crashed onto one of the accommodation areas, killing an anaesthetist while he was asleep. Otherwise the staff were coping magnificently, and had plenty of supplies as well as support from the military, so we left a few hours after we'd arrived.

On our way back to the airport, I saw what was left of the cinema: a few seats in the rubble, and a door frame. Leaning up against the lone frame was a large piece of cardboard. On it someone had written, 'Now Showing, Gone With The Wind!'

We were told that many shocked and panic-stricken people had taken off in their vehicles, naturally wanting to put as much distance as possible between themselves and Darwin. Police and military personnel were concerned that many of those fleeing the scene would have insufficient fuel, water, food and first-aid supplies to see them through—which is why Alice Springs was on alert, preparing to receive large numbers in need of food and shelter. It was the height of summer, so the oppressive heat was an additional danger.

The people of Alice rallied round magnificently. Women cooked huge amounts of food, made copious sandwiches, and opened up their homes for families to stay. Boxes of clothes were collected and distributed. Many of the refugees, particularly those with young children and babies, were too frightened to spend a night in Alice, fearing the cyclone would strike again there. They took food and water, and carried on down to Adelaide, despite the police trying to convince them to stay put. Little children clung tightly to their white-faced mothers. A number of people, particularly young parents, were mute with shock, unable to speak without bursting into tears. The fear registered on their faces was awful to see.

Several women had gone into premature labour and were admitted to the hospital. A few men had chest pains, and many people had minor cuts and bruises, but it was the sheer terror of what they had experienced that had left its mark in the immediate aftermath of the cyclone. The hospital, while disrupted for a day or two, thankfully did not have to deal with the large numbers of injured people they had expected.

Gradually things settled but, as much as a year later, people who had been in Darwin that Christmas and were now living in Alice Springs were often unable to talk about their experience without weeping, or stammering, or trailing off in mid-sentence. Those that did speak of the disaster told of the indescribable power and sound made by the wind.

There were funny stories too. One man described combing through a three-storey apartment block, reduced to matchsticks by the cyclone, to search for a friend with whom he had been drinking the day before. His pal, who lived on the top floor, was still fast asleep, oblivious to the fact that his bed was now at ground level!

That was one Christmas those involved were unlikely ever to forget.

20

Pride and Prejudice

My relationship with Matt continued to fill most of my off-duty time. Of an evening we'd go to the folk club where we'd first met; and, happily for me, Matt got on well with Aalbert and Ingrid, who we would see occasionally when they came into Alice. (Less happily, a few years later Ingrid wrote to me with the news that she and Aalbert had divorced and she was back in Holland, with their two sons.)

We were still exploring the canyons, gorges and chasms of the Red Centre, and of course, marvelled at Uluru/Ayers Rock. I never climbed the rock, choosing instead to walk around the base, marvelling at its sheer size and the changing colours as the sun dipped below the horizon. I instinctively felt that it seemed like trespassing and not quite right to trek up the well-worn trail to the top of what was known to be a sacred site in the

Dreamtime stories, although hundreds did it every day.

I was closer to the indigenous people than Matt was; after all, I met them daily in my work, and came to know some of the mothers and their little children on my visits to the creek camps. I tasted witchetty grubs when they were offered, but only those that had been briefly cooked in the hot ashes of the campfire. Not wriggly live ones. No sirree!

They tasted good, like almonds, as I'd been told they did.

I also sampled morsels of lizard and goanna, offered to me by Susan. They too had been baked in the ashes of the campfire and tasted fine, a bit like stringy chicken.

Out in the bush, kangaroo hunting was men's business. The kangaroos I saw several times in camp had been shot. Pick-up trucks loaded with a family or two would take off looking for the herds of red kangaroo. The women and children in the group usually wandered off with their digging sticks to find lizards, goannas or rabbits. On finding fresh burrows, the digging stick would be pushed into the ground nearby, and the animal's track followed with the stick until it could be dug out. The women were known for their skill in this.

Matt and I enjoyed a warm, happy relationship for the first two-and-a-half years or so that we were together, sharing many of the same interests and, of course, our adventures. But then, one Anzac Day, there was an incident that made me begin to ask myself some tough questions.

Anzac Day commemorates the 25 April 1915 landings of ANZAC troops at Gallipoli during World War One, and is now the date when

Australians remember their dead in all wars. In 1976, veterans marched, as usual, through Alice Springs and up to the memorial at the top of Anzac Hill, overlooking the town. That is where we joined the congregation of townspeople for the remembrance service. Matt had a particular interest that year as two of his American work colleagues were Vietnam veterans and had been invited to join the march.

As we stood in the warm sunshine, joining in the moving ceremony at the memorial, I noticed, standing some way away and quite apart, a middle-aged Aborigine lady and two younger men. One of the men was swaying on his feet, clearly somewhat inebriated, but all three had the hymn sheet and were quietly taking part in the service despite appearing to have distanced themselves from it.

It bothered me that this little trio were so separate from everyone else, so I moved over and stood next to them for the remainder of the service. This caused lots of people to turn and stare at me, some with curiosity, others with open disdain.

Matt pretended not to notice and stayed where he was. A different version of the thousand-yard stare, I guess you could call it.

The Aborigine lady, who had come from Pupanya, told me her name was Susie and the two men were her sons. By now the inebriated one had stepped backwards, too close to the edge of the hill, slipped, and had rolled halfway down the slope. We carried on singing.

When the service was over, just as I was about to introduce Matt to Susie, he grabbed my arm and tried to manoeuvre me away. 'What the hell

172

do you think you're doing? Haven't you got any pride?' he hissed.

I said I'd see him later, as I was staying for a while. He was furious, and others I knew just walked past me with a curt nod and no acknowledgement of the people I was with.

So much for sharing and caring.

Susie told me her brother had been killed in Vietnam eight years before. 'We came to sing to him here, instead of at Pupanya.' Tears slid down Susie's cheeks, and I walked slowly down the hill with her as she told me more about her brother. In her pocket she had his medal, which she took out proudly to show me. I was so touched by her story, and so ashamed of—and angry at—all the others. What the hell was wrong with people, I silently asked myself. Even when supposedly reflecting on the folly of war and paying their respects to the dead, there was another kind of war going on all around us. I just didn't get it. And I still don't ...

*　　*　　*

Matt and I had our first heated argument that night, and I started seeing him in a different light. He was raised in rural Texas, and prejudice was beginning to show.

One time I wanted to watch a film made for television called *The Autobiography of Miss Jane Pittman*. Cicely Tyson, one of my favourite actresses, was playing the part of an indomitable black civil rights campaigner, Jane Pittman, born into slavery in 1850s Louisiana and surviving into the 1960s. I had read the Ernest Gaines novel on which the film was based, which included the

173

powerful scene where an elderly Pittman drinks from a 'whites only' water fountain.

Matt was furious that I wanted to watch this film with a couple of friends, rather than spend the evening with him. He was determined that I should not watch it, and I was equally determined that I would. What the hell was such a big deal? I asked him. Was it maybe that he was scared of facing his own prejudices? That went down well! I tried encouraging him to stay in and watch it with us, so that we could have an adult debate about it afterwards, whereupon he erupted.

'You think I'm interested in a nigger woman who drank from a white fountain? I am not,' he said quietly, maintaining eye contact. That was somehow more chilling than if he had ranted and raved.

I think that was the final nail in the coffin for me. Things were never quite the same after that particular clash of wills.

In retrospect, I wondered why it took me so long to pick up on Matt's biased attitude. Maybe it was part of the slow unravelling of an affair that had run its natural course, but it was hard to know because, whenever anything remotely of this nature arose, we clashed badly.

I couldn't imagine how I had failed to notice his behaviour for almost three years.

Well, they do say love is blind ...

*　　　*　　　*

However, much earlier than—and in total contrast to—Matt's outbursts on Anzac Day and about the Jane Pittman film, he shared the great excitement

174

in Alice Springs when it became known that Charley Pride, the country and western singer, might be coming to give a free open-air concert in the town's Pioneer Park. It was unheard of then for a major star to deviate from the well-trodden Sydney–Melbourne route, where concerts easily sold out. No stars of note bothered to trek up to Alice Springs, which was then well off the beaten track, but Charley wanted to sing for the Aborigines in the outback.

As soon as the concert was confirmed, just three days prior to the Thursday date, the excitement was palpable. Matt was keen to go, and nothing would have stopped me. Truckloads of Aborigines began arriving in town from the surrounding missions and cattle stations, and even the squatter camp in the riverbed hummed with chatter about the 'black like us' singer who was coming to town.

Charley Pride was born in Sledge, Mississippi, in 1938, one of eleven children of a sharecropper. Charley bought his first guitar from Sears Roebuck mail order when he was fourteen and taught himself to play. Meanwhile, he joined the Negro American Baseball League and played for the Memphis Red Sox. By the 1950s and '60s, he realised he would not progress far in baseball. Fortunately, his greater talent lay in music, and he went on to land a recording contract in Nashville when the rich quality of his silken baritone voice began to be heard. His colour was kept a secret for the first three years of his recordings, but his talent overtook prejudice and he is still the only Afro-American country and western singer to be a member of the Grand Ole Opry.

Just before dusk on the day of the concert,

175

along with hundreds of others, all armed with blankets and pillows to sit on and beer on ice in our faithful Eskys, we converged on Pioneer Park, a large area of grassland where local sports events—everything from Aussie rules football to horse-racing—were held. A large wooden stage had been erected at one end, with lighting, microphones, amplifiers, etc. Many hundreds of Aborigines were sitting quietly on blankets laid out on the grass. The entire area was soon filled with expectant faces shining with excitement.

When Charley Pride sauntered on stage, strumming his guitar and addressing the audience, we all went bananas, whistling, applauding, cheering. Interestingly, the reaction of the Aborigines was quite different. They sat silently, gazing in awe at this tall Afro-American man dressed in a black suit with sparkly bits and fringing on his jacket, almost disbelieving that a man of colour could command such fervour and excitement.

The music was beyond great: 'Crystal Chandeliers', 'Ramblin' Rose', 'Mississippi Cotton Pickin' Delta Town', 'Kiss an Angel Good Morning'. Out tumbled the favourites.

We loved every single minute of it and sang along until our throats gave out. Charley gave encore after encore—he sang for several hours. After each number, the Aborigines, silent at first, began whispering reverently, 'Charley ... Charley ...' It was as though they could scarcely believe that he was singing for them. After a while, with beer cans and 'puckin' plagons' emptying, they began applauding and cheering like the rest of us in the crowd. That good-natured, magical concert was such a wonderful experience, and I loved watching the people of the Red Centre relishing this completely new experience for them in 1970s Alice.

Charley Pride must surely have felt the love rolling towards him that night.

*   *   *

Papa Luigi's was the only Italian restaurant in Alice. The food was excellent and the atmosphere cosy and intimate. No wonder, then, that it was very popular, and we often dined there.

One evening, a group of us celebrated someone's birthday at Luigi's, and left at about 11 p.m. Amid cheerful goodbyes, 'see you guys tomorrow' and lots of hearty laughter, we made our way across the well-lit main drag to where our vehicles were parked, when we became aware of a young Aboriginal woman of mixed blood, cursing loudly and drunkenly. But it was what we saw her doing that shocked us. In either hand she held a broken liquor bottle, and she was slowly and systematically grinding the glass into the side panels of every vehicle parked in the street. The damage she was doing was methodical, extensive and difficult to watch—her concentration, determination and intense level of anger were chilling.

The women in our group instinctively wanted to help stop her, as much for her protection as for the preservation of the vehicles, but the men said, 'Keep away, she'll only turn on you.'

Witnessing her raw hatred made me realise that beneath the surface of this beautiful land there

177

were huge issues that were simply not being addressed. What I saw in her young face was not just the consequence of heavy drinking. There was more than one generation of suppressed fury and frustration.

The police turned up and threw her forcibly into the back of a wagon, taking her off to who knew what fate ... Perhaps we would be seeing her in the hospital next day.

*   *   *

Like many of the doctors and nurses at Alice Springs General, I was frequently asked to volunteer at various events—which is how, one winter, I became a first-aid attendant at Aussie rules football matches at Pioneer Park on Saturday afternoons. I covered three games before I gave up. Running onto the field with a bucket of iced water and sponges to tend sweaty players rolling around in the agonies of cramp, I felt like a self-conscious prat.

Spectators thought we knew what we were doing, but we did not.

Another event I volunteered for was the endurance horse race, then held annually. The local vet approached me in the ER to ask if any doctors or nurses would be interested in being invigilators, and I managed to rustle up six of us. The race was split into fifteen miles for juniors and thirty miles for adults, and prize money was significant enough that risk to the horses' health could not be ruled out. Hence the need for extra invigilators at checkpoints. After instruction from John, the equine vet, I was assigned to the fourth, penultimate, checkpoint.

Juniors were aged fourteen and younger. Their ponies or young horses did well, with no unpleasant episodes, but the adult (largely male) riders were single-minded in their pursuit of the prize money.

As each horse thundered into the checkpoint area, we had to check heart rate, respiration rate and rectal temperature. After a twenty-minute rest period, the same observations were recorded. If the readings had not dropped to within the specified safe range, animal and rider were disqualified. When galloping in, the horses were covered in lather, foaming through their nostrils and generally suffering from very rapid, disordered heart and respiration rhythms. Deciding to disqualify someone invited a range of anything from abuse from the rider to the offer of a bribe.

I found the whole experience extremely distressing and never volunteered again.

I was, though, reasonably happy to attend as a first-aider at the twice-monthly rodeos held at Ross River homestead. Here, both horses and bulls were ridden, usually bareback. The Aboriginal stockmen excelled and were a joy to watch; they became as one with the animal, demonstrating with ease their complete mastery of conquering and controlling the magnificently powerful beasts.

I was surprised to see young teenagers, including girls, riding bareback on the bucking broncos. The first time I attended, I was a mass of anxiety. Some riders hit the ground with a wallop, and were barely visible through the clouds of choking red dust. Each time, I prepared to go into the arena thinking they must at the very least have smashed a bone or three, yet the hapless rider would invariably jump up, dust himself down, spit out a few teeth, and remount.

I was learning the hard way that life was far more relaxing in this part of the world if one did more spectating and rather less volunteering!

*   *   *

Our time in Alice was drawing to a close. After a final Christmas spent with good friends, in early 1977 Matt and I went to Los Angeles together to spend some time with friends and family. We had shared some very good things together, but it was nearing the time for both of us to move on.

The trips we had taken outside Australia over the years would never be forgotten either. Particularly memorable was the 1976 Winter Olympics in Innsbruck, Austria, where we sat four rows from the front in the ice-skating stadium and marvelled at John Curry winning his gold medal. How different is the real experience from watching these events on television. We fought our way up a mountain to watch Matt's beloved men's downhill event. Standing thigh-deep in snow with hundreds of others, we sipped glasses of spicy mulled wine to keep alive, and with tingling toes and ruddy cheeks, basking in the warming alcoholic haze, we were enthralled as the world's top skiers zoomed down the almost perpendicular slope in a blur of testosterone.

Another very special, very different experience was our trip to Normandy. Matt was a great World War Two buff and had always wanted to retrace the Normandy landings. We walked along the windswept beach at Arromanches, where the remains of the Allies' artificial Mulberry Harbour can still be seen; and, wrapped up against the bracing January winds, we walked the length of what are still referred to as Utah and Omaha beaches, where so many American servicemen were slaughtered. Gold was where British lads died, Canadians were mown down on the Juno section of beach and young French and British killed on Sword. I was astonished at how like the North Wales beaches of my childhood they were.

Following an unmarked trail among the dunes, we had stumbled upon the American military cemetery, unseen from down on the beach. We looked at the symmetrical rows of white crosses in stunned silence: almost 10,000 dead American servicemen lying in orderly, frozen precision, so that we should never forget. The familiar feelings of compassion, respect, sadness and anger surged through me, choking me with emotion. I said nothing to Matt, who was caught up in the honour and glory of it all, living his dream.

There were other vacations, other good—and not so good—times, but my free spirit was champing at the bit and Matt had to return to his work in Los Angeles. Reality was setting in.

But I have to mention how, on one visit to Los Angeles, we were invited to a party through Matt's sister, Frances. Frances was a trusted employee of Cesar Romero, the Cuban-born 'Latin lover' movie star of the 1930s, '40s and '50s, and the party was to mark his sixty-seventh birthday.

The celebration was held on a balmy evening in the extensive grounds of a mansion in Pacific

Palisades. A Mexican mariachi band in colourful, intricately embroidered *charro* suits strolled across the lawns, serenading the jovial gathering. Twinkling lights threaded through trees and scarlet blossoms bobbed on the surface of the large swimming pool. Impossibly handsome waiters circulated with silver trays bearing cocktails—including my favourite, margaritas. And the food, especially the *ceviche* of raw fish marinated in the juice of limes, was spectacular. Frankly, the whole thing was like a scene from one of Cesar Romero's glamorous movies of the 1950s and seemed quite unreal.

I was dazzled by it all, but tried not to behave like a starry-eyed fan or stare at the famous faces I recognized. Mr Romero, though, took a bit of a shine to me, mainly because he 'just loved my English accent': 'That's so cute, say that again.' Then, this elegant, graceful man, quietly instructing me to say nothing to anyone, asked me to station myself near a small wooden side gate at the far end of the grounds, and wait there. A close friend, he told me, would be coming along in about ten minutes' time to wish him well, but didn't want a fuss and would only be there for a few minutes. And he would like me to meet this unnamed woman.

Somewhat bemused, and a little nervous, I did as he said, and leaned against a tree, sipping my margarita and wondering who on earth was going to arrive. After a few minutes, Mr Romero, with the party's photographer and a couple of other people, arrived at the gate in time to see a limo pull up.

What happened next was a moment I will never

182

ever forget for, with her trademark young hunks, one on each arm, the mystery visitor appeared. Mae West! Long blonde hair, sparkling diamond earrings cascading from each ear lobe, heavy ice-like glitter at her neck, and rocks on every finger. She smiled from scarlet lips, as Cesar Romero advanced and kissed her hand in best Latin lover fashion.

It's not every day that you see such an iconic figure up close, and I was transfixed.

It was as I marvelled at her strapless, deep purple gown swathed around her body in swatches and folds, and at the fichu of almost transparent froth surrounding her shoulders and arms to her elbows, that I noticed the elbow splints. And realised that the inanely smiling young men in evening dress on either side were actually supporting her, taking her full weight as they held firmly onto the splints. Her feet barely touched the ground. As Mr Romero placed a cocktail glass in her hands, which did not move, I saw that her rings were clipped onto fingers cruelly twisted by arthritis. The long platinum hair of legend was several 'falls'; the eyelashes were false, as were the long, scarlet fingernails, and I realised I was looking at a very fragile 80-year-old lady.

The nurse in me saw all this, and wished that I had not. She was trapped in her own legend, and the years are unforgiving. I could also see that this was how she wished to be remembered.

She was Mae West after all.

A couple of photos were taken and then she was gone, leaving only a trail of her wonderfully exotic perfume, and an image in my mind that I wasn't sure I wanted.

I remembered how, when I first saw the pyramids of Giza in Egypt and the Taj Mahal in India, I had been initially transfixed by the sights so familiar to me from photographs. Then, when actually there, you see the slums of Giza nudging up against the pyramids; the shocking vandalism of graffiti carved into the exquisite marble of the Taj.

Perhaps, I thought, that night in LA, icons should remain in the pages of school textbooks or movie magazines.

Three days after that party, Frances came in waving a magazine and we all looked at the photographs of the glamorous gathering.

And then, there she was—Mae West, laughing into the camera, looking like—well, Mae West. The hunks, the diamonds, the gorgeous gown ... all there as always.

This great lady died a few years later at the age of eighty-seven.

How about that.

Part Three

CHANGING GEAR

Sea Views

For years I had harboured a dream of learning to sail, really sail. I had spent the odd day with friends on their boats, just enough to whet my appetite, but now seemed like the perfect time and place to seize the moment.

After Matt and I had brought our time together to a close with a sunset picnic on Santa Monica Beach—there's nothing quite like a fine, chilled Chablis to take the edge off that dull ache that settles around the heart, no matter how right the decision is—I turned to the pages of the *Los Angeles Times*, where large numbers of sailboat owners regularly advertised for crew. I was interviewed by Jim Bridges, the grizzled owner of a beautiful 50ft ketch called the *Fantasy*, and was taken on as the only woman member of a crew of five.

On 2 March 1977, we set sail southwards from San Pedro marina on a misty early morning, bound for Central America and the Caribbean. Jim's dream was to winter in the Greek Islands, then return to California across the Pacific. Most crew members were youngsters trying to get somewhere else and offering their sailing skills in return for a free passage.

Jim was a wealthy retired businessman with all the time in the world to do as he wished, and the expensive boat, filled with all kinds of superfluous but impressive gadgets, was his pride and joy—

along with his young blonde companion, Lori. Sadly for Jim, Lori jumped ship in a haze of cannabis in Acapulco, never to be seen again. But he still had his beloved boat ...

I quickly settled into the disciplined routine required to sail under canvas, and over the following six months I discovered a natural and easy affinity with life on the ocean wave, learning to read charts, taking my turn on watch, and doing much of the cooking on the small, gimballed stove, mainly because I was better at it than the guys!

The next few months passed in a kaleidoscope of colourful adventures. We stopped and went ashore wherever the mood and the winds took us, from poor Mexican fishing villages to the playgrounds of the famous and the very rich. We explored the west coast of the Baja; crossed the Gulf of Tehuantepec, which had inspired Jules Verne to write *Twenty Thousand Leagues Under the Sea*, and where I saw my first hammerhead shark racing ahead of us in the crystal-clear waters. Elizabeth Taylor and Richard Burton must, I thought, have been insane ever to leave the romantic beauty of Puerto Vallarta. But while ashore in El Salvador, we became horribly aware of the tensions simmering beneath the surface: in the beautiful whitewashed square of San Salvador, we watched in horrified bemusement as young men were rounded up and pushed into the rear of trucks, their anxious womenfolk looking on in silence. We did not stay there for long.

On through the Panama Canal, and a few days anchored in the San Blas Islands, where we met the proudly independent Cuna Indians who inhabit eight of the some 370 islands that form this archipelago off the coast of Panama. The turbulent Caribbean was very different from the laid-back waters of the Pacific, and we had warnings from various coastguards and other sailboat owners to guard against drug-dealing piracy.

One afternoon, en route to Cartagena, an unidentified vessel showed up on radar, following us for some time until we were able to see it with the naked eye. The seas were choppy, the winds strong, so it was difficult for the boat to draw alongside. Frighteningly, the grey cutter had no markings, no flags, and the six bearded men on deck looked a motley crew. They wore no recognisable uniform, just dark pants and a variety of T-shirts. They drew closer and instructed us to drop sail and prepare for their boarding. Jim ordered me down below, with instructions to stay there.

Though there were no firearms on board, Jim's hand was hovering over the flare gun to be used only in emergencies at sea. That scared me more than anything else. I watched through the porthole as three of the men came aboard, two of them armed. I locked myself in the small head, or toilet—as if that would fool them ... I could hear them demanding to know who we were and to see our papers. This was seriously scary. After a tense exchange between the men, relieved laughter broke out, and Jim called down, 'You can come out now, Anne. It's OK.'

It turned out these guys were members of the Colombian Guardacostas, operating undercover just outside Colombian waters, hunting for pirates. I thanked them for scaring the living bejesus out of us before making them mugs of tea. They warned

189

Jim to remain vigilant, and to be aware of how vulnerable our boat could be. They were nice guys, and escorted us into Cartagena where we bought provisions, made some repairs and tasted the local nightlife with two of the coastguards who owned a local nightclub as a sideline. One of them taught me to samba: those snake-hipped men can move like no others. You'd better believe it!

*　　　*　　　*

Next stop was Jamaica, where we dropped anchor for three weeks off the pretty little coastal village of Port Antonio. Here, the locals taught us how to curry goat's meat and make delicious plantain soup; here, too, we danced till we dropped at the nightly village reggae band hop, and took a two-day trek into the Blue Mountains to see where the famous coffee is grown.

One night I was last to leave the village dance and found myself stranded on shore, looking across the small harbour at the *Fantasy* anchored some 600 ft away. It was 3 a.m., a bright moon lit up the sparkling water—and all the dinghies were gone. I asked one of the police officers standing nearby if he would mind my purse and shoes, which I would collect from the police station later in the day, and keep watch while I swam out to the boat. Laughing, he agreed, and I struck out, following the light of the moon on the water. I squelched up the ladder and lowered myself through the hatch into my small cabin and quickly fell asleep.

Three hours later I was rudely awakened by the sound of gunfire close by. Poking my head up through the hatch—the other crew members were doing the same thing—we saw two police speedboats travelling in small circles around the bay. It was 6.30 a.m. and dozens of women were gathered, as usual, on shore where they washed their clothes. What was not usual was their shouting and frantic pointing at something in the water, which the police were randomly peppering with rifle fire. Apparently one of the women said she had seen a crocodile swimming close by those who were knee-deep in their washing chores—a most unusual sight because crocodiles are freshwater creatures. Voodoo was alive and well in 1970s Jamaica, and stories abounded of 'spells' being placed on people who were out of favour. Many thought that the sighting of the croc was just a wild story—until the police dragged the body of a large crocodile they had shot onto the nearby beach.

I was paralysed with shock by this incident, remembering that barely three hours before I had swum back to the boat in that very bay. This was the rainy season in the Caribbean and each morning there was a short, sharp, fierce downpour of tropical rain, which left everything steamy and humid. The theory was that the local river had become swollen with water, and this crocodile was washed down the swirling waters and out into the bay.

It was quite a few days before I was able to explain my sudden uncharacteristic reluctance to enter the water. Jim got very worked up when I confessed, and forbade any of us to swim after dark.

Next, we made our way to Florida via the

Cayman Islands. By now we had taken a good six months with our adventures, and I was getting restless, beginning to miss nursing and eager to get back to it. I had always known that my sailing career was only an interval before I returned to my first love. And, since there was never a shortage of good, healthy young people ready to take over and crew, I decided to leave the boat at Fort Lauderdale.

Six months on board the *Fantasy* had sometimes seemed just that: a fantasy. A wonderful experience during which I'd not only learned a new set of skills and seen much more of the world, but meeting the owners, passengers and crew from other boats had taught me that sailing encompasses people of all nationalities and backgrounds, and is far from the prerogative of the idle rich.

But Jim wanted to spend a few months in Florida before pursuing his dream of sailing to the Greek Islands, and I knew that hanging about and administering the occasional bit of first aid for minor ailments and injuries was no longer going to be enough. This seemed an opportune moment to return to my chosen reality and, with a good friend about to be married in Vancouver and Canadian family to visit, I decided to make for Vancouver as a staging post on my next, as yet unknown, professional journey.

I travelled by Greyhound coach—quite a contrast to the boat—and arrived in good time to attend the wedding, meet up with friends and generally find my land legs again.

* * *

Back from my sailing trip and visiting family on Vancouver Island, I was struck by the contrast between the vibrant colours of life throbbing throughout central Latin America and the Caribbean, in all its glorious messiness, and that of the sedate, conservative charm of retired folks in this manicured corner of British Columbia.

One day, in downtown Victoria, I was being treated to the famed English afternoon tea served at the Empress Hotel by some friends (shades of Sri Lanka!). No one in Britain had seen such teas since the days of the Raj, and then only the well heeled, but that was irrelevant given that gullible tourists were paying $35 for warm scones served with heavy cream and strawberry preserves, along with dainty crustless sandwiches of smoked salmon and egg and watercress, so synonymous with the refinements of old England.

It was here that I first heard the story of Judy Hill.

Judy Hill was one of two nurses caring for a community of some 420 Inuit people in Spence Bay (now called Taloyoak). Accessible only by air, or the annual supply sea lift, the settlement lay 290 miles east of Cambridge Bay and 760 miles northeast of Yellowknife on the Great Slave Lake. It was not unusual to find British nurses or midwives manning health centres in isolated Inuit communities dotted throughout the Arctic. Our British training in the 1960s and '70s, particularly of midwives, placed such nurses in great demand.

On 8 November 1972, Judy had been responsible for the care and safe transfer of two patients requiring urgent medical attention to the base hospital in Yellowknife. David Kootook was a fourteen-year-old boy with an acute appendicitis and Neemee Nulliayok was heavily pregnant but with complications. The party of three was flown to Cambridge Bay, where they had to change planes. A Gateway Aviation Beechcraft 18 had just offloaded three prospectors and was immediately available for charter to Yellowknife.

Martin Hartwell, the bush pilot, agreed to medevac the group and the small plane took off in heavy weather and temperatures of minus-35 °C. En route, the plane crashed into a hillside, killing Judy on impact, with Neemee dying a few hours later. Martin Hartwell sustained fractures in both legs. David, uninjured, was able to erect a makeshift tent and find firewood.

Thirty-one days later, the pilot was found alive, but in a mentally rambling state. David had perished from a ruptured appendix one week before rescue. The pilot had beaten death with the help of the stricken boy and by eating flesh taken from Judy's leg and buttock.

The news spread rapidly and was shocking in the lurid detail so loved by the tabloid press.

David and Neemee were laid to rest in Edmonton. Judy's ashes were scattered on a quiet section of the beautiful Bow River near Banff, by her boyfriend, Chris.

Soon afterwards the Judy Hill Memorial Scholarship was set up to help fund nurse training for Inuit and other students and is successfully functioning today, nearly forty years later.

This touching story piqued my curiosity about what lay to the far north of this vast country. Despite others warning me that 'there is nothing up there. You'll be bored stiff', I knew I wanted to see for myself how the remarkable Inuit survived such a brutal, isolating climate. I resolved to go, and contacted the British Columbia Nursing Registry in Vancouver to see if there were any nursing vacancies in the Arctic.

22

Eskimo Point

I was told about a temporary position that was about to be available for some eight months at a traditional Inuit settlement called Eskimo Point. It was on the western shores of the mighty Hudson Bay, in the Keewatin zone of the Arctic. One of the two nurses stationed there would be going away to attend a course in Halifax, Nova Scotia, leaving a vacancy to be filled—and an opportunity for me to 'dip my toe' into the Arctic experience.

Employed by Canadian Health and Welfare, I would be one of two registered nurses manning the health centre at Eskimo Point, and expected to deliver a full spectrum of health care to 1,600 Inuit people. Ten days later I flew up to Churchill, Manitoba, to take the three-day 'Introduction to the Arctic' course provided for government employees.

Here, with two other British nurse/midwives and two young Canadian schoolteachers, we learned that Inuktituk is the spoken language of the Inuit who, for thousands of years, passed on their heritage through legends and song. With the

195

coming of missionaries in the late nineteenth century, a written form in syllabics was introduced in order to spread Christianity and the teachings of the Bible. By 1978 English was taught in government schools on the settlements, and most young people under twenty-five spoke English. Each health centre was staffed with young interpreters drawn from the community. We were taught how to withstand and respect—but not to fear—the hostile climate we were about to experience; learn how to live with it, and to acquire some of the skills honed by the people who had survived it for many generations.

The busy base hospital in Churchill was the lifeline between the isolated settlements, and we were shown how to use the short-wave radio to seek advice or call for assistance in an emergency. I was instantly reminded of the School of the Air and the Royal Flying Doctor Service in Alice Springs, which linked the vast distances of arid desert between the hardy, resourceful inhabitants scattered throughout central Australia. The only difference now was that the endless desert was a permafrozen tundra. Those radios truly were a lifeline in every sense.

We were advised on appropriate clothing and footwear to protect us from the approaching winter, and kitted ourselves out at the local store. My parka hood was trimmed with wolverine fur, the recommended first choice for effectively protecting the face from the dangerous wind-chill factor. Inner and outer jackets, trousers, mittens and boots were purchased at subsidised prices.

The pharmacist at Churchill gave us a detailed rundown of which medications we would have at our disposal to prescribe and dispense. More unusually, we nurses were taught how to take diagnostic X-rays on the very basic machines we would find in the health centres, and we spent an afternoon in the pathology laboratory learning how to prepare samples of blood, urine and other bodily fluids into smears and slides for microscopic examination. These are not normally tasks carried out by nurses, but by radiographers and pathologists; in the isolated Arctic, however, such basic diagnostic processes fell to nurses because it was not at all cost effective to staff every isolated health centre with a full complement of clinical specialists.

Every six weeks, we were told, a doctor would visit each station to hold a clinic for two or three days, following up on any cases referred by the nurses or seeing anyone requiring a private consultation. The system was efficient and well thought out, and we were reassured to know that there was fast and efficient support available at all times via radio from the mother hospital. Anything of a more serious nature and the patient could be flown out, or an appropriate doctor flown in.

We spent a day beyond the town, out on the tundra, learning how to cut snow blocks, build sheltering walls, dig a snow cave, and generally get the feel of the elements surrounding us. I was fascinated by the almost crystalline quality of the air. It felt like the cleanest air I could ever possibly hope to breathe, yet it was so cold that to inhale deeply would risk freezing the lungs. I watched as my breath, caught in the characteristically long hairs of the wolverine, immediately froze and rapidly formed a protective mask of ice across my face. The wind was shut out and I could see ahead of me, but within fifteen minutes I had to break the ice mask in order to clear my vision. I quickly realised that I was encountering a whole new dimension of Mother Nature.

Though Churchill has always been noted for the large numbers of polar bears who gather there in the summer months, by early November they were heading out to their hunting grounds as the Hudson Bay froze up, leading them out onto the pack ice where they wait patiently for seals to gather at their breathing holes. I didn't get to see any bears then. That would come later.

After this induction course, we three nurses were ready to set off: I to Eskimo Point, one of my colleagues to Rankin Inlet, and the other to Baker Lake. We wished each other well and said our farewells.

*　　　*　　　*

Eskimo Point lay some 100 miles north of Churchill. The settlement was only accessible by air, by boat only during summer months, and—as I was to learn—by an extraordinary machine called a Bombardier that ran on a caterpillar-track system and looked like a tank. It was able to transport eight passengers, who had to endure an ear-splitting noise inside this bone-shaking vehicle. I flew.

Arrived at my destination, I stepped from the small plane onto what passed for a landing strip, feeling like an overstuffed turkey in my bulky Arctic clothing. Despite that protection, the cold wind clawed at my skin, ripped off my hood and

198

literally took my breath away. The Inuit hunter alighting behind me quickly pushed my hood back onto my head and told me not to let go of it for even a second, or my ears would freeze. I could barely hear his words through the wind that howled around us. He took my elbow and steered me into the shack a few steps away.

I felt stunned by the onslaught of elements I could not have imagined in my wildest dreams—or nightmares.

The hunter introduced himself. 'I am George Igoolik,' he said. 'My wife Susie is the clerk/interpreter at the health centre. I will take you there, and she will give you hot tea and much information. You must be careful not to lose your hood or your mittens. Your skin will freeze and you will lose fingers and ears.'

No kidding, Sherlock!

It was colder than a mother-in-law's kiss out there, and I couldn't see a thing. That the pilot had landed the small plane was testament to his skill.

The door of the shack burst open and in blew a tall man dragging a large bag. This was John Wilson, the sole RCMP officer who manned Eskimo Point. He welcomed me, laughingly saying his pregnant wife, Gwen, would be relieved that the new midwife had arrived safely. George bundled me and my bags out to his waiting truck and, negotiating his way through swirling snow and poor visibility, drove me to the health centre that would be my workplace and my home through the long winter ahead. We clambered up a steep flight of wooden steps, through a double-door system and into a small, wood-panelled lobby leading to a small desk. The room was warm, cheerful and more homey than clinical. I felt like the mythical Yeti who had been blown—unprepared and befuddled—into a different world.

A smiling brunette in smart white nurse's uniform moved towards me, hand outstretched. 'Anne, welcome. Sorry I couldn't come to meet you, but we have three croupy babies in oxygen and Millie is in labour. Thank God you're here! Oh, by the way, I'm Dorothy!'

Such was my introduction to my new adventure in a land that was perhaps the furthest removed in climate and in culture from any I had ever known.

23

Caribou Nights

The weather was so bad for the next forty-eight hours that I neither ventured outside, nor could I see what lay beyond the windows of the nursing station. It was like living inside a snowball. But inside we were warm, cosy and able to carry on with routine work.

The ever-cheerful Susie, our Inuit clerk/interpreter, turned up like clockwork each day, staggering through the double-door system covered in snow, hood pulled well down over her smiley face. Nor did the raging elements deter Henry, our health care assistant and interpreter. Henry stood maybe five foot in height, spoke quietly and only when necessary, and was a good man to have around. His skin was dark and weather-beaten, with even darker patches, characteristic of the older men—the mark of having been exposed to the harsh environment for so many years. Despite his caribou (known as reindeer outside North America) parka and the fur hood pulled over his face, Henry also wore tinted goggles. He told me he had suffered snow blindness a few years earlier and now took extra precautions to protect his eyes. He never removed the goggles immediately on entering the building, but allowed some five minutes or so for them to thaw out and loosen their frozen grip on his face.

Dorothy Milkovitch was my age, late thirties, and of Ukrainian origin. The largest group of Ukrainian immigrants had settled in the prairie provinces, and Dorothy was born and raised in Manitoba. She was a brilliant nurse and I learned much from her. She had a collection of delicately hand-painted eggs, and taught me the intricacies of the traditional patterns. Her mother had embroidered a beautiful shawl for her that was another example of the traditional skills learned in the 'old country'. We both lived at the health centre, in comfortable quarters at one end of the building that reminded me of the hospital in Cassiar, but on a smaller scale. We had a bedroom each, shared a comfortable sitting room and a sizeable kitchen, and there was an extra bedroom provided for visiting doctors.

The labour room was well laid out and equipped; two examination rooms led into a large treatment room; the small laboratory and X-ray room, together with a cosy waiting area, formed the bulk of the station, while a little room leading off the office housed the precious short-wave radio transmitter.

201

On the morning of the third day the weather cleared and I was able to look out of the windows at the settlement. Small, wooden houses painted in cheerful pinks, blues and yellows were scattered around, seemingly haphazardly, looking for all the world like the 'hundreds and thousands' a child would sprinkle onto the icing of fairy cakes. All dwellings were built on sturdy blocks, raising them several feet off the permanently frozen ground. Even in what passed for the short summer months the tundra was solid with permafrost. In order to ensure the oil-heated homes kept warm, and were kept free from the deep snows of the long winter months, they had to be raised off the ground. The space beneath provided shelter for the teams of huskies that huddled outside most dwellings.

Every house had several large blocks of ice stacked outside. I learned that when water was required indoors someone, usually one of the women, came out with an axe, with which she energetically attacked an ice block, filling a container with the glistening shards. This in turn was thawed and heated in a large pot on the oil-fired stove. The men went out onto the tundra, a distance from the settlement, to cut the blocks. Out there the snow was clean and the ice pristine, untainted by the dogs within the settlement and safe to drink.

Eskimo Point lay within the Keewatin zone of the Arctic. At that time, 1978–9, the settlement had a population of some 1,600 of whom only about ten people were not Inuit: Dorothy and myself, of course, the RCMP officer John and his wife Gwen, and an engineer called Bill who took care of everything else that was beyond the reach

202

of the rest of us! The remaining members of the non-indigenous group were teachers at the school.

The winter rapidly deepened around me as I familiarized myself with the routines of caring for this traditional Inuit settlement. Apparently, the word Eskimo means 'eater of raw meat'. Here, the people were heavily dependent on the vast caribou herds in particular, but also on whale, seal and walrus. Some caribou herds wintered around Eskimo Point at that time: their skins were used for clothing, their meat eaten—raw, of course— their antlers and bones used to make utensils and tools. Nothing was wasted. Seal, walrus and beluga were hunted at Whale Cove, a short distance north, as well as from the Hudson Bay itself. Seal meat is high in Vitamin B12 and iron, and sealskin—strong, waterproof and hard-wearing— was made into boots, parkas, and harnesses for the dog teams. Seal oil was used for cooking and in oil lamps. The huskies are magnificent animals with luxuriously thick coats and curly tails that fold neatly along their backs. Their power, enjoyment and high spirits when pulling the *komatiks,* or heavy wooden sleds, are legendary, and that source of energy needed feeding. Seal and caribou kept them going too.

I was initially surprised at the generally low blood-pressure readings and healthy haemoglobin counts of the Inuit women who attended our ante- and post-natal clinics. There was no doubt that the diet of high protein and low unsaturated fat worked in their favour, despite the absence of sufficient fresh vegetables or fruit, which was hardly available. The small—and only—Hudson Bay store stocked a limited amount of pathetic-looking peppers, potatoes and greens at extortionate prices. Otherwise provisions were tinned.

I was impressed with the organization of the health centre, Dorothy's competence and the hardy residents of Eskimo Point. This was an experience like no other. We worked twelve-hour shifts, dealing with all aspects of mother-and-baby care, with vaccination programmes and school health, the treatment of illnesses and the administering of first aid. The small radio station—or Arviakpaluk as it was known in Inuktituk—was a godsend. Every home had a radio and we could broadcast any messages we needed or wanted to communicate to our patients. It was a fast and efficient way of making sure they knew when to come for their clinics, when the visiting doctor was arriving and so on.

Something I quickly discovered was that some of the Inuit use a form of facial sign language. A very slight, almost imperceptible raising of the eyebrows means 'yes', and an equally slight, split-second wrinkling of the nose means 'no'. I chanced on this while examining a young woman who was complaining of severe abdominal pain. As I carefully palpated, she made no sound, and I asked Susie if she felt pain. 'She is saying yes, she is feeling pain ... she is telling you no, not there ... here ... it is painful.'

After a couple of minutes of this I said to Susie, 'But she hasn't said a word. I need her to tell *me*, not you.'

And that was how I learned to recognize the very faint facial signs that the poor girl was giving me. Not once did she cry out in pain, but she ended up being flown down to Churchill, where they removed her inflamed appendix that same day. The women were stoic in childbirth also, and it was a pleasure to deliver their babies.

* * *

The days were shortening rapidly and by Christmas time there was only a couple of hours of softly indigo daylight. The sun barely rose before sinking below the horizon.

The biggest health problem we encountered that winter were chest infections in babies and toddlers. Families lived close together in the small, overheated little wooden homes, where often one large mattress on the floor was where everyone slept. Sharing everything is an integral part of the Inuit culture but, unfortunately, this meant infections spread quickly.

Many babies were prone to croup, and we often had to admit them overnight as their coughing reached alarming levels of distress. Dorothy and I frequently split our work, one of us taking a twelve-hour day shift and the other twelve hours through the night, in order to give optimum nursing care around the clock. When several babies were in the centre at one time it was the only way we could cope.

In those days it was common practice to nurse babies and toddlers in an oxygen tent draped over the cot and tucked firmly under the mattress. Through a small side flap in the tent we would insert the nozzle of a steamer, giving the child a constant flow of oxygen and warm, humidified air to soothe the terrible paroxysms of coughing. This combination was always effective and rarely did we need to administer antibiotics for croup.

Bronchitis was a different matter. If a high fever persisted we advised antibiotics, but we were always sparing with them, knowing that to give such drugs 'prophylactically' demonstrates poor practice. Sadly, today it seems most children, as well as adults, in the developed world have been given antibiotic therapy ill-advisedly, hence the rise of the 'super bugs'.

We aimed always to teach and include the mothers in all treatments and decisions made about their children's healthcare, and to teach them how to cope and administer care. We also regularly visited patients in their homes. In the late 1970s, TB was still prevalent among the elders of the community and the treatment—a combination of the drugs streptomycin and rifampicin—was required daily for nine months. These elderly patients were generally unreliable in taking their medication, so part of our daily visits was to ensure the tablets had been swallowed.

On visiting an Inuit home, you generally entered a scene where a few women were sitting in a circle on the floor, raw liver in their white teeth, chattering and laughing uproariously while butchering several caribou. The floor would be slimy with blood as fresh livers were thrown into one corner, antlers in another, intestines in yet another. Raw liver was a great delicacy among the Inuit, and Nellie, one of my patients, would always greet me with a cheerful 'Hello, Sister, you want some?' while offering me a hunk of fresh, warm, raw liver balanced on her curved *ulu*, the traditional blade the women used for their task.

206

'No thank you, Nellie,' I would always reply. 'You know I am trying to give it up!' That always made the women laugh, no matter how many times I said it.

This little exchange was always followed by an offer of tea. I soon knew not to accept until I had checked whether there was a pot of water already bubbling away on the stove. If so, I would say yes; if not, I declined the offer. I had learned this the hard way: the first time I entered an Inuit home and was asked if I would like a mug of tea, I immediately said yes, whereupon Gracie rose from her haunches, put on her parka and boots, grabbed an axe and a huge pot, and went out into the snow.

That is when I learned what the mysterious blocks of ice were for. Gracie hacked efficiently at the block, then placed the shards of ice into the pan. Back indoors, the pan of ice was placed on the stove until the resulting water was heated, then tea leaves and lots of sugar were tipped into the pot and the brew stewed for fifteen minutes. When ready, the tea was poured, with great ceremony, into chipped tin mugs, and strangely delicious it was too. It's amazing to think how the simple ritual of making and drinking tea is part of the comforting and welcoming of strangers the world over.

*   *   *

I was invited by William, one of the hunters, to accompany him on a caribou hunt one day. I had mentioned to Henry that I would like to go, and I was very fortunate to be asked—especially since it seemed to me, after I was instructed to keep as

207

quiet as a mouse, never speak, just watch and learn, that I was being taken along on sufferance. Good old Henry could fix most things!

Muffled up against the cold, I sat to the rear of the large, wooden *komatik*, which was pulled by a team of eight dogs. William urged them on with a loud clicking sound of his tongue made through clenched teeth. Not many words were used, but the man and his dogs were as one. I remember fearing we would get lost in what was, to me, a complete white-out. The settlement was well above the tree line, with nothing to break the horizon. This was dirty grey-white tundra, extending as far as the eye could see beneath a sky of the same colour, with no visible horizon. Suddenly, all one's familiar terms of reference were gone, and with them one's sense of perspective.

The course instructor back in Churchill had spoken of this phenomenon: he had explained that if ten-gallon oil drums and cans of beer were both painted black then scattered over a wide area during such a white-out, it would be difficult to determine which was a large drum a few hundred yards away and which a beer can up close, as perspective is absent. It was very disorientating, and I began to understand what he had meant. Not even a compass could be of use because we were located too close to the magnetic north.

About half an hour into our journey, I looked anxiously behind me. The settlement was out of sight, and we were entirely surrounded, indeed smothered, by the whiteness. My eyesight and hearing were excellent, but next to William I was as if deaf and blind. Every now and again he would bring the dog team to a halt. Then he would almost sniff the air and feel the wind on his cheek, listening to sounds I couldn't hear. After some time, though I could still otherwise see nothing, suddenly—as if springing from a child's pop-up picture book—right ahead of us, there was the herd. Hundreds of reindeer, just standing quietly looking at us.

Signalling for me to stay exactly where I was, buried snugly beneath some pungent caribou skins, William grabbed his rifle and began walking slowly towards the animals. I was astonished to see that not a single one of them moved. It was as though they were offering themselves up as a sacrifice. William peered down the high-powered telescopic lens of his rifle and selected the animal he was about to kill. I felt like standing up and shouting, 'Run, run. Get away.' Just like we did as children in Wales all those years ago, trying to save bunny rabbits in a field of corn.

I looked on in amazement as the shot rang out and one of the magnificent beasts immediately crumpled and fell to the ground. The herd members closest to the fallen one shuddered and shifted a bit, but stayed where they were. William took aim and shot a second animal. As it fell, its antlers clanged against the antlers of its mate on the ground.

Temperatures that day were forty-five below zero, just like a deep freeze. William cut off the legs of his kill, strapped the two corpses across the front of the *komatik* (but partly on my feet and knees), and back we went to the settlement. I felt exactly the same as I had when, on holiday in Spain years before, I went to a bullfight in Barcelona. You know exactly what is about to happen, but when you actually see it with your own eyes it takes on an otherworldly feel and the shock plays the horror of it back to you in slow motion.

That was how I felt about that adventure. It was shocking and distressing yet, as is so often the case with time-honoured traditions, there was a sort of majesty about the fatal encounter.

*   *   *

Most of the first aid we administered involved the suturing of lacerations or treatment of burns and scalds. Children who had fallen and banged their heads warranted a stay overnight in the health centre, so we could observe them for vomiting or unusual drowsiness, the early signs of concussion. Fractured limbs or bad sprains were not unusual, particularly on sports days. The young men often played games that tested physical prowess such as wrestling or—more unusually to us—trying to kick a piece of bone suspended a good six to eight feet above the ground. Simple fractures were straightforward to X-ray and stabilise with a cast until the next visit from the doctor, who would check it out. If Dorothy and I were concerned or unsure about some of our diagnoses or decisions we called up the base hospital in Churchill. They would advise, or send a plane to transport the patient to them.

The biggest suturing I ever did was to stitch on an ear! George, who had met me on my arrival, was one of the most respected hunters in the community and one of the few at that time who owned a Skidoo. Out speeding along the tundra one day, he hit a hidden bump and went flying up in the air. As he came down, his face was caught by the Perspex windshield, which sliced into his left cheek and almost severed his ear from the side of his head. He managed to sort himself out, packed snow around the wound, and got himself to the health centre, where I attended to him.

I could see that, luckily, the cut was pretty clean, not ragged, and no tissue had been gouged out. So, nothing was missing; it was just a case of sewing his ear neatly back to where it belonged. Just . . . ?!

I was a bit nervous at first. I had no wish to disfigure George for life, and the procedure took me absolutely ages. However, it all came together quite easily and George thought it was hilarious. He sat looking at himself the whole time in a hand mirror that his wife Susie brought in! I can honestly say this was the only time I ever gave someone a course of antibiotics 'just in case' it got infected. The doctor was arriving in three days' time, so by then we would be able to check out the wound. Well, it healed like a dream, and George said I had made him 'even more good-lookin', Sister'.

They breed 'em tough up north.

*   *   *

Most of the hunters were older men, and most hunted with dog teams. The up-and-coming generation of younger men preferred to speed over the tundra on the backs of their souped-up Skidoos. There were not many in 1978, but it was clear to see that the traditional hunting methods were about to be challenged. We can't stop change, not even in this isolated part of the world.

I had a long chat one day, over several steaming mugs of sweet tea, with one of the older hunters, Sammy Alouak, when I went to visit his sick wife, Nellie. He said the young men do not understand the value of dogs. The dogs sense danger and will never take you close to the floe edge; they can, and will, find the settlement in a white-out; they can retrace their steps; if the weather closes in, dogs will keep you warm. Less happily, he also told me that if you are in big trouble and the risk is frostbite, you can kill a dog and warm your hands in its belly.

A Skidoo can run out of gas if you get lost. A Skidoo will take you into water when visibility is poor. The younger men rely too much on machines and are losing their tracking skills. If you hit the water you are dead in seconds. It has happened to some of their young men, Sammy said, staring with his rheumy old eyes into the middle distance as he puffed on his pipe of tobacco.

It was sad to hear all this, but each generation will always seek to find its own ways, make its own mistakes. 'Twas ever thus.

*　　　*　　　*

One night in January I saw the aurora borealis like no other I have ever seen. The curtains of colour that danced above us were indescribably beautiful and made me want to cry with the wonder of it all.

To those who said, 'What are you going up there for? There's nothing up there,' I answer, 'How wrong you were!' I would wish for everyone to experience such beauty before they die. Despite man's blundering through the natural world

212

around us, this is surely one phenomenon that he will never be able to taint with his presence.

Then, one April morning in 1979, while trudging through the softening snow on my house rounds, I saw a small flock of little snowbirds. They were the size of English robins, but snow white. Something in the air was changing, as though God had flicked a big switch somewhere. I thought for a moment I was hallucinating, but I was actually observing the first sign of spring. Over a few days the walkways loosened into slush then turned into shallow lakes, and a few patients paddled to the centre in kayaks. That's how sudden the thaw was.

Sadly, it was soon after this that I had to leave Eskimo Point. The nurse I had been relieving was ready to return, and I needed to get home to see my father. He had always enjoyed my letters, vicariously sharing in my travels and adventures by reading about them, but now it was time to go home. At least for a while ...

I left with only a couple of disappointments. While I was in Eskimo Point, I never got to see the waters of the Hudson Bay. They were frozen solid the whole time that I was there, with sailing boats and whalers stuck fast until the short summer would burst upon them and free them up for just four short months. And I never got to see a polar bear either. They were well away from the settlement and hunters seeking them out were away for several days at a time.

As I took my leave, I felt sure that I would return one day to see what this isolated, magical place might look like in summer.

Part Four

THE YEARS BETWEEN

24

Family Matters

I would indeed return to Eskimo Point one day, and to Cassiar in the Yukon, and to the Red Centre of Australia, as I eventually returned to Vietnam. There would be many new and as yet unknown experiences and adventures in my ongoing quest to know the wider world, to try and understand its many different peoples and cultures and, above all, to care for those in pain whoever they might be.

At that moment, however, April 1979, I knew that the time had come to return home to Wales for a while, relearn how to live in a more 'ordinary' environment, and catch up with friends and family, particularly my father.

By now my father had sold the hotel where I had passed so much of my youth. He and my stepmother, Edith, lived in a pretty cottage in the small Welsh town of Denbigh, where I spent from late spring to early autumn with them. Edith remained as cold and distant as ever and her constant nagging distressed me, but my father seemed unfazed by it and I realised that this was just how their relationship was. All in all, it was a happy time for me and my father, though I could see the years had begun to take their toll on him. I loved sharing my traveller's tales with him—and even with Edith, who had her own sadly unfulfilled dreams of distant lands.

I helped my father with his gardening during the

217

spring weather and, in being with him daily, came to realise how alike we were in certain ways. Daddy was fascinated to hear my descriptions and see my photos of Eskimo Point and its Inuit inhabitants, and even more interested in all the details of my sailing trip. Former naval man that he was, he would talk with me about those adventures for hours on end, his eyes misting over with nostalgia at hearing how his 'errant' daughter—which is how he thought of me—seemed to be retracing his own adventurous steps. Coming from his background and generation, he had never (and would never) come to terms with the fact that the world he had known was changing around him. It confused him that a daughter would do all of this; he never did quite understand why I hadn't toed the party line of earlier decades, which was to marry and have children.

There was one great sadness for me during this visit, one that reinforced my belief in how much better life would be if only parents would talk to their children openly, honestly and from the heart. It was a lovely August day and we were out weeding my father's beloved garden. The sun was warm on our backs, birds twittered cheerfully in the trees, and together we were enjoying a quiet and peaceable moment that had presented itself. I knew I had to seize that moment.

My mother's death had never, ever been mentioned after it happened. My sister Susan and I had been sent away from home, and Mother died in our absence. I had been barely ten years old at the time; I was now thirty-nine. So, at last, I broke the long years of silence and asked my father what had really happened to her. It was a big mistake.

218

His face turned an alarming purple, his eyes bulged and his clenched, white-knuckled fists were clamped to his sides as, clearly lost for words, he spluttered, turned on his heel and stomped up the garden and down the street. I felt frightened. The look on his face was an indescribable mix of sorrow, shock and fury. He was gone for some three hours and I knew better than to try and follow him. When he eventually returned he was calmer.

Neither that incident, nor my mother, was ever referred to again.

My father died on Easter Sunday, 1985. The many tears I wept were not only the expression of my bereavement, but for the realization of how much I had wanted to tell him and ask him, how much was left unsaid. Now it was too late. He must have gone to his grave riddled with remorse, guilt and some confusion.

*   *   *

After so long a period of opting out of work and travel, and having relished catching up with family affairs and enjoying seeing my sisters and brothers, the old restlessness that always crept in when I took a break began to surface. I knew it was time to move on again.

Once more, it was the Save the Children Fund that provided me with an opportunity to help make a difference to the suffering of mothers and children who found themselves the victims of politically driven tragedy.

So it was that I took fond leave of my family and flew off to Thailand, the first of many journeys and jobs in parts of the world very different from the one I'd left behind me in the Arctic wastes.

25

Comings and Goings

In October 1979, as the human tragedy of Cambodia unfolded on the Thai/Cambodian border, I responded to a request from the Save the Children Fund and travelled to Thailand to be part of a team in a refugee camp called Sa Kaeo. Not since Vietnam had I witnessed suffering on such a scale; particularly distressing among the more vulnerable mothers with babies, and the larger numbers of orphaned or unaccompanied children who had fled the cruelties of Pol Pot's regime in Cambodia.

I was unprepared for the scale of the humanitarian disaster unfolding in front of me in my first few days at the camp. On my arrival, I was dropped near to a field that was covered by a mass of blackness for as far as the eye could see. I slowly realized that I was staring at thousands of black-clad people lying on the ground, all too ill or fragile to move. The stench was indescribable but the strongest memory I keep is the eerie silence of the place. There were no human sounds to be heard. No coughing, no babies crying, no murmur of voices.

Many died within the first few weeks or so. It was as though, having found a safe haven, such damaged bodies and souls could cope no longer. Exhausted by their ordeals, often brutalized beyond healing, their bodies ravaged by disease and man-made famine, they just quietly slipped away.

But nothing stays the same, and the situation moved on. In time, while the weakest died, the survivors grew stronger, and slowly but surely the camp began to take on a life and character of its own.

Our schedule was tough, working twenty-one days straight. There was no electricity in the camp, so teams worked from sunrise to sunset. On two occasions, vehicles carrying casualties, including young men with bullet wounds, arrived at dusk just as teams were departing. Quickly, Red Cross ambulances and other vehicles were driven into a semicircle, their headlights providing light for doctors to assess the condition of the patients.

Throughout this, a well-planned camp was being constructed from bamboo and thatch around us. After ten days, an amazing 38,000 people were moved in and accommodated in blocks, each of which comprised twenty huts.

Everything always seems to have its up side. The initial indescribably appalling conditions in the sprawling camp were quickly improved by the expertise of the UNHCR, the Red Cross, and the many international organizations, including the always impressive Médecins sans Frontières. They were helped by the generosity of people the world over who donated in so many ways, and a group of superb women who left their privileged lives in Bangkok to work as volunteers. Many of those refugees were given immigrant status to Canada, and are now contributing to society in a variety of distinguished careers.

The border camps remained in place in one form or another until 1995, when the last one finally closed. Those still living there at that time were repatriated to Cambodia.

(I have written more fully about my time in Thailand in my first book, *Always the Children*.)

*   *   *

I returned home for Christmas 1980, but by February 1981 I was again off on my travels and broadening my professional—as well as cultural and geographical—experience. This occupied me for the next twelve years, spent largely in the Middle East.

First stop was Egypt where, in a complete change of gear professionally speaking, I was appointed Nurse Administrator at Al Salam International Hospital in Cairo, a shiny new facility on the banks of the Nile. There was no military war to fear here, only the shocking situation of the downtrodden. I loved the Egyptian people and the magnificent ancient sites and landscapes of the country, but the yawning chasm between ostentatious wealth and grinding poverty I found distinctly unpalatable to be around. On completing my two-year contract, I took my leave without too much regret.

I was recommended for a position at the new 300-bed Hariri Medical Centre in occupied South Lebanon. This was a truly sobering experience, witnessing the horrors of the Arab–Israeli conflict at first hand, and I wondered yet again why we don't realise that, though cultures, religions and ethnicities seem to separate us, we're really all the same beneath the skin.

I would have these thoughts, and despair of politicians and stereotyping, again and again, as work took me to Saudi Arabia, Kuwait and Abu Dhabi. Along the way, I witnessed the ravages of the first Gulf War, and lived with the zealotry that so defines the lives of the women of Saudi Arabia. Despite having an open heart and an open mind about different religions and cultures, I found some of Saudi Arabia's customs neither pleasant nor easily justified.

As a nurse, you have a window onto the intensely private world of each patient. Despite many families being wealthy, some of the young girls we met had not been educated about their bodies and knew nothing of menstruation. Their lack of knowledge was matched by their lack of opportunity. In Saudi Arabia, women were only allowed out in public with a close male relative and forbidden to drive, vote or socialize outside the home.

Even in the face of the injustices I witnessed in the Middle East, those years were a magic-carpet ride through many different cultural experiences. The common thread, as always, was the decency and kindness of ordinary people.

*   *   *

In 1985 I returned to Britain and took an intensive three-month course in management before taking up a post at a nursing home in Battersea. There I oversaw the conversion of a local, badly run

223

council home for elderly people into a well-run, privately owned establishment. The Dickensian horror stories of what I found in that institution gave me an unhappy perspective on the belief that the care of the elderly provided at that time in Britain was superior to that in so many other countries.

* * *

I had long resolved to revisit Canada and Australia, and see how the Native Americans, the Inuit and the Aborigines were faring three decades on. So, in 2009, I boarded a plane for Whitehorse and began my journey of rediscovery.

26

Return to the Yukon

In July 2009 I returned to the Yukon. Would it have changed much: indeed, had *I* changed much? My perception of everything might have altered: forty years is a long time.

The start of my trip was not altogether auspicious. At Heathrow I had treated myself in the duty-free shop to a perfume I normally could not afford, only to have it promptly and permanently confiscated by security staff because it was 10ml over the accepted liquid limit on flights. Seriously, would a terrorist hell-bent on mayhem be wafting Chanel's sexy 'Chance' around the terminal, I argued? No—they did not buy that argument. Rats! They have their job to do.

Several other passengers had their bottles of water, bought in the departure area, confiscated also. I was furious at the apparent lack of joined-up thinking that allowed such items to be sold within the departure area, and can but hope airport authorities have rectified this blunder of selling such dangerous items to the unsuspecting public!

Horse and stable door come to mind ...

Nowadays there is the sheer boredom that has come to characterize airports over the years since my first youthful and exciting journeys when everything was a novel experience. Having endured Heathrow, when we touched down at Vancouver en route, I was again reminded of the pressure to buy stuff you don't need; to eat food you don't like because it passes the time; anything to kill the tedium of waiting to get somewhere else.

All that was forgotten as my plane approached Whitehorse. I stared out of the window at the sparkling Yukon River meandering timelessly below, evergreen forests crowding in on its emerald water, and my dormant memory of the majestic beauty of Northern Canada was instantly reawakened.

After a perfect landing I made my way across the blistering tarmac and into the terminal building. There she was, my ebullient cousin Sally, smiling and waving.

I had first seen Sally, the youngest of five children in her family, as a dimpled, mischievous, tow-haired child in Vancouver some forty years previously, and then again when she had visited London ten years before this meeting.

The speed at which the years had whizzed by

225

gave me quite a jolt, but the discomforting thought was lost in a tangle of hugs and laughter. I had finally returned to the beautiful wilderness but, not having slept for some twenty hours, I experienced everything through that artificial adrenaline-fuelled alertness that simultaneously heightens the senses yet puts one at a remove from everything.

As Sally drove me downtown in her adorable little Smart car, most of the traffic was made up of huge trucks, dented pick-ups, SUVs, and the vast, sleek recreational vehicles, or RVs, so beloved of retired Canadians and Americans. These gas-guzzling monstrosities spread along the Alaska Highway like a gleaming metal rash, many driven by baseball-capped senior citizens. A number of these travellers looked like they could use some life support but were nevertheless determined to strike out into the wilderness, kidding themselves they were roughing it like the pioneers of yore.

The Smart car makes a clear statement that requires no words.

Sally's handsome French-Canadian partner, Paul, welcomed us home with bear hugs, and we talked and laughed for hours over a delicious meal, served with slabs of warm, home-baked bread and copious amounts of red wine. It was still light when, at midnight, exhaustion overtook my excitement, and I finally crashed and drifted off to sleep.

Over the next two weeks, we caught up with the news of the past forty years, like you do, helped by Yukon Gold beer and the unfettered love, merriment and sheer joy that flows between good friends and family, despite absences and the cruel passage of time.

Sally and Paul are dedicated environmentalists whose determination to cherish and preserve our beautiful planet is reflected in their every action, a way of life I quickly grew to respect.

During my visit, Sally explained how, in the mid-1980s, aged twenty and with a college degree in forestry, she had hitchhiked to the Yukon, instinctively drawn to the land of wilderness and opportunity. However, when she saw the size of the trees she quickly dropped the idea of a career in forestry, but loved the purity and simplicity of life in the quiet north so much more than the urban rat race. I recalled how, on her visit to London, the proximity of everything in our cities had shocked her. How could people live like that? she had said, wondering at the crowds, the cars and the houses jammed together, cheek by jowl.

I've wondered the same myself on many an occasion.

Sally describes herself as being an environmentalist for practical reasons. The lifestyle is non-consumerist, efficient and inexpensive. With less money needed to live, the more wealth of time there is to enjoy life and its surroundings. Like me, she considers her most sensible choice was to have no children. 'There are quite enough humans on the planet, why would I wish to contribute to the problem?' she says.

For myself, I have seen at first hand how many children on this planet have no one left to love them. Maybe people like me were put here for the purpose of filling that loveless vacuum.

Sally and Paul enjoy challenging the status quo, taking satisfaction from actually living the dream rather than just talking about it. Their peaceful, low-octane life, using solar power and driving a tiny car in the land of oversized vehicles, filled me with an envious longing to follow their example (even though, in my own small way, I do try not to extract from Mother Earth more than I put in).

* * *

Some 200 miles northeast of Whitehorse lies the gorgeous Kluane National Park. Here, Sally has realized her dream of building a home of logs that is at one with the land. She constructed it herself, taking five years to complete this beautiful structure that sits a pebble-throw from Kluane Lake.

She chose to build it using the stack-wall technique because the size and shape of the logs makes it easier for a single woman to manage the construction. Paul and a few friends helped only with the pouring of cement for the floor slab, and the roof construction. Embedded into the walls at intervals are variously coloured glass bottles which light up at different times of the day, depending on the time of year. It is like living inside a sundial, or a poor man's stained-glass window. Yellows signal breakfast time, blues light up at noon, and red heralds the mellowness of evening.

The only trees cut down to make space for this wonderful retreat were those already standing dead, having been attacked by the massive spruce-bark beetle infestation that began in 1992.

I stayed at the 'tree' house for three days. It felt as though the dwelling grew out of the ground, and I absolutely loved it.

The only aspect of the experience that made me

gulp were the toilet facilities, situated a distance away from the house, along a winding trail through scrub and trees. Inside a basic wooden structure, over a hole some six feet deep, the throne sat in solitary splendour, its three surrounding 'walls' draped with one of Sally's own silk-screen works of art. When sitting on the comfortable wooden seat of this eccentric arrangement, one gazed at an eye-wateringly beautiful mountain range, fringed with trees that pressed in on all sides.

I was strongly advised to sing loudly when walking the trail to and from the loo, in order not to suddenly startle any bears that might be around. What about me being startled, I asked? I might not make it as far as the bloody throne!

Fresh water was hauled from the lake every few days, a chore that was usually left until evening. At that time of year, the blissful peace and beauty of the surrounding mountains, the flashes of characteristic fireweed cutting pink and red swathes along the banks, and the turquoise waters of the lake softly ruffled by a summer breeze were magical. From the sandy shore, Sally surveyed her kingdom, dragging behind her the little wooden cart with its two large bicycle wheels that she had made, which carried a five-gallon drum ready to fill from the lake.

'You want a beer?' asked Sally, when we'd collected the water.

I should have known she was ready for any eventuality. 'Hold on,' she said, walking a few feet away from where we stood. Then, from behind a bush she dragged two small canvas beach chairs and from a small hole in the ground, covered with a lid, produced two cold cans of Yukon Gold. Now that's what I call a great pub—there just when you need it!

We sat there, sipping our beers, and watching the light move and change over the landscape. This was living, and Sally had found her special place.

*   *   *

Back in Whitehorse after this little idyll, I spent time walking around this dusty, pioneering town. It was hot, in the mid-thirties. While shops and businesses had changed over the years, basically the town felt pretty much the same, though in deepest winter it looks more pristine lying under many feet of snow in the crackling, sub-zero temperatures.

The entire Yukon, I was surprised to learn, has a population of only 33,000 people, of whom 25,000 reside in Whitehorse. Britain, with its population of 62 million and rising, could easily be placed within the borders of this state, with room to spare. A sobering thought.

I was relieved to find that the time-honoured festivals and fun days were still celebrated in these parts, offering a release valve for the tough Yukoners. The Sourdough Rendezvous, Yukon International Storytelling Festival, Dog Sled Races and the feisty Frostbite Music Festival were going strong, plus countless others. I would need a year to tackle all this wonderful stuff on offer. For those who dismiss the north as being 'space with nothing up there', which I heard from so many city dwellers in the south, I say try it—you'll like it!

The indigenous citizens are now known as the

First Nations people. I saw only a few around the town. At a small playground I noticed a giggling knot of young children playing on swings and a roundabout, drawing shapes in the dust, and generally busying themselves doing stuff that five-year-olds do. Their chubby, rosy-cheeked innocence echoed the laughter and games of children everywhere in the world. Some of these kids were First Nations, others were of mixed ethnicity, but all played happily together.

By contrast, further down the street, loud verbal abuse was being hurled around among a small group of older First Nations people, remonstrating with a young couple who were slumped on the kerb; stale alcohol smells wafted around this sad tableau. As I walked past, I caught the eye of one of the women, so I smiled a 'good afternoon'. She responded, her voice slurred, with 'Fuck off, you fucking white bitch', and continued in a drunken incoherent mumble. I turned into a nearby store that sold nothing I was remotely interested in. It seemed sensible at that moment.

This distressing and disturbing incident happened at four o'clock on a sunny afternoon. Clearly, the anger of the group was directed not only at each other, but at whoever walked past and probably the world in general.

That fury was palpable, and I immediately remembered the feelings of impotent rage that came over me so many years ago in Qui Nhon as I watched a Vietnamese child, ten-year-old Ba, and a nineteen-year-old American soldier on a plane, with not a leg between them. The feeling that life is desperately unfair to some makes you so bloody mad, yet you don't know who to be mad *at*—and that adds more to your fury. It's not a good feeling, and it is exhausting.

I got the distinct impression that what I had just heard and witnessed was a vignette of that type of rage.

Happily, though, despite those whose lives are ruined, things have moved on for many. The First Nations are now self-governing and have authority over their land, acquired through land claim negotiations.

Running the gamut of employment opportunities, small native-owned businesses and large development corporations are both in evidence, and there are plenty of success stories— for example, Air North, the small airline which is 49 per cent owned by the Gwitchin tribe of Old Crow. There have been, and are, problems along the way, particularly in the cyclical nature of the boom-and-bust mining industry; nevertheless, land claims have transformed the Territory, and the Yukon is seen as a model of how to get it right, despite consumerism snapping at its heels.

But there is a large segment of the First Nations people who carry the burden of recent history with them as they move into the white man's twenty-first century.

A woman who illustrates to all of us the residual baggage of a time when church and paternalistic government colluded to 'take the native out of the child for its own good' is Connie.

Her extraordinary story, which I recorded on tape in July 2009, was made all the more shocking by her insistence that it is a very common story among the indigenous people of Canada (and I mean all over Canada, not only in the Yukon).

Connie, a friend of Sally and Paul's, dropped by one morning with her friend, Julie, to say hello over a cup of coffee. The first, and immediate, thing I noticed about Connie was the expression in her eyes. Not the thousand-yard stare exactly, but the intelligence mixed with pain. This look was familiar to me.

We talked much that morning, and this tall, slim woman, with her straight blue-black hair falling from a central parting either side of her strong face, opened my eyes to a shameful part of recent history. Everything surrounding her early life she has researched over several years.

Born in Prince Albert, Saskatchewan, Connie was taken from her mother, a Cree Indian named Veronica Cook, at birth. The cord was cut and Veronica was told that her baby had been stillborn. Father was not around, and Connie was given to an Anglican minister and his wife. She never found out whether money crossed palms at that time.

Raised as a little white girl, Connie was sexually abused by her adoptive father until she was about ten years of age, when he lost interest in her. She told me, 'He liked very prepubescent girls.'

At this time the family moved to Fiji. Up until now, everyone in her world had been white. Now she was seeing people who were black and brown. Classmates asked her how come this white couple had a brown child. Eventually, she plucked up the courage to ask them and was told she was adopted. They sent her to the minister's family in the West Country, England, to complete her education. Here, cared for by her aunt, she attended a private girls' school, where she was labelled a Paki both by classmates and people in the streets.

Of this period, she said to me that 'Neo-Nazis were alive and well in 1970s Britain', which made me squirm. At the time Connie had had no idea what 'Go home, Paki' meant, and didn't discover the origins of the insult until a few years later. She was deeply unhappy and, by the time she finished at school, had been away from Canada for eight years. So, aged eighteen, she returned to the country of her birth, but not to her adoptive parents, and began to research her roots.

Over the years, she discovered that her mother had given birth to eight babies, three of whom had been 'apprehended at birth' and adopted. Connie was one of them. She learned that many First Nations babies were sold 'south of the border', with $5,000 being the going rate. This practice was quite common until a law was eventually passed in the mid-1960s prohibiting it.

According to official registry figures, the number of babies apprehended at birth was 36,000, but it is estimated that a more accurate figure would be closer to 80,000 over a ten-year period.

To sit opposite a person who is looking you straight in the eye while telling you of this suffering inflicted by others, it is difficult to know what to do with the anger and compassion that threatens to overflow.

Over the years Connie, unsurprisingly, fell victim to drug and alcohol addiction, has had several brushes with the law as a result and spent time in and out of rehab. Although her anger and pain are clearly visible in her eyes, her demeanour and her writings, today she lives with her friend and partner Julie, and has a grown-up son whom she adores.

Connie is, today, a person of some note. She writes poetry—as she so rightly says, grief and love both make for great poetry—and has published four books. She travels around giving poetry readings, happy to do so as her cultural roots are firmly nomadic.

I can't forget her saying to me, quite sincerely, 'I don't know why you are so interested in my story. It is the story of so many of my people.'

Bloody horrifying, I call it.

*   *   *

Sally was happy to drive me to Cassiar, the original focus of my return to the Yukon. Both saddened and inspired by my meeting with Connie, I faced the coming trip with a mixture of hope and apprehension.

27

Ghost Town

Early morning, and the midsummer heat was already pressing in as Sally and I enjoyed a mug of freshly percolated coffee. Sitting out on the back porch, watching the rise of a sun that had barely set, we talked about the trip ahead of us that day, anticipating (in my case with a heart that beat faster at the thought) the 220-mile ride down the Alaska Highway, through breathtaking wilderness beauty. Then turn right at Watson Lake and drive another ninety miles to the mining town of

Cassiar—or what might be left of it since the boom in the asbestos market had turned to bust.

The Smart car, tiny and space-efficient, was loaded with our two small holdalls, a five-gallon jerry can for extra fuel, drinking water, and a huge bag of carrot sticks and apples to nibble en route. We were set to go.

I knew this would be an interesting trip down memory lane, and possibly a bit sad too. I knew that Northern Canada was littered with the scarred remnants of mines that no longer served their original purpose—basically that of yielding obscene profits for a moment in time—but Cassiar was the only such one that I had experienced at first hand and, from what I'd heard, I expected to see some sort of ghost town.

Every now and again, as we bowled smoothly along the paved Alaska Highway, an enormous RV would zoom past, its occupants tooting their horns at the little Smart car as they went, sometimes in scornful disbelief, but usually in amazed admiration.

During the long drive to Cassiar, Sally and I found ourselves with a precious stretch of unbroken time, just the two of us together and undisturbed, in which to share family stories, tell terrible jokes, and discuss the life lessons we each had learned. Though of different generations and raised on separate continents, Sally and I, both free and independent spirits, discovered we are alike in a number of ways. Certainly, we shared a sense of despair about the wear and tear on the planet, caused on the one hand by greedy exploitation, and on the other by the ever-increasing numbers of human beings seeking a warm safe habitat, enough food, and clean water.

Our knowledge of, and concern about, these difficult matters were in stark contrast to the thousands of acres of wilderness we beheld on our journey. We saw lakes where an occasional moose could be spotted, wading slowly through placid waters and sending a sparkling wake of ripples to nearby grassy banks. Mountain ranges fringed the horizon, and I marvelled at the sheer scale of still-unspoiled landscape all around us.

Inevitably, in my mind's eye I remembered with absolute clarity the large mobs of people hanging onto the overcrowded trains in India; recalled the poverty and hunger in Calcutta that turned children into scavengers; saw the misery of Kibera, near Nairobi, where well over a million destitute live with open sewers and zero hope. As I looked on the beauty around us and remembered these things and more, I found myself on the verge of tears, almost weeping with frustration at the gross mismanagement of this, our beautiful Earth.

Where, I said, voicing my thoughts to Sally, are the leaders, the movers and shakers with vision? One day the poor and dispossessed will rise up in a swell of raging hopelessness and helplessness, railing against those with the gilded mansions, the luxury yachts and private planes, who drape their women in blood diamonds from the profits of defiling our God-given resources. It was, of course, ever thus. I would have thought we might have learned something by now, but as Sally said, and she is right, each one of us can only do whatever we can, wherever we are and with whatever we have, to improve the lot of our fellow men.

Perhaps, if we all did just that, the world could

237

be a better place.

*   *   *

Finally, we arrived at Watson Lake. Only another ninety miles to go! We stopped there for a break, and yes, there were the place-name signposts, but not as they were in 1966. Now there were hundreds, with many more stored in a warehouse nearby. Diane, who ran the tourist shop, grew very excited when Sally told her of my putting up the Welsh village sign all those years ago: LLANFAIRPWLLGWYNGYLLGOGERYCHWYRNDROBWYL LLLANTYSILIOGOGOGOCH.

As a young girl of nineteen, Diane had just started working in Watson Lake, and still remembered the jovial group that arrived from Cassiar to nail this extraordinary place name up on the posts. She said it had been up for years and was much photographed by tourists, but eventually it had weathered badly and was now 'somewhere with all the rest' in the warehouse. We laughed fondly at the memory of that warm sunny day, the quantities of cold beer that kept us going, and our pride in our handiwork.

I reminded her of how I'd had to get my father to send proof that there was such a place name before the sceptical sheriff would give me permission to put it on display. Now anyone and their dog was tacking up all sorts of signs—some not too polite. Nothing stays the same, I guess . . .

We struck off on the last stretch, down the Cassiar highway. Over the years, the road had been paved and there were no more giant trucks loaded with asbestos barrelling past us and kicking up clouds of dust. But the glorious scenery was unchanged and this was still bear, moose and curly-horned mountain goat country. The lakes and rivers would still be jumping with salmon and grayling, and autumn colours would still be spectacular. Good Hope Lake on our left made me chuckle as I remembered the buxom German lady water-skier who ended up with the huge wooden sliver in her ample buttock! We were maybe four miles from where Cassiar town site had been.

A few scattered log cabins on either side of the road looked a little forlorn. This is where my friends had lived in the mid-'60s. There was no sign of anyone and the cabins had an abandoned air about them, suggesting there was not much activity in the area. I thought of Melvin Pete and his daughter Mary, and hoped that perhaps their children and grandchildren were still there, out fishing, or hunting—or maybe working up in Whitehorse.

To my astonishment, as we rounded the last bend we were confronted by the tailings pile. It was a good three times larger and higher than it had been in the 1960s, a green mountain that, as we drew closer, was oddly beautiful and spine-chilling in equal measure.

Brightly coloured wild flowers grew at the base of the once toxic pile, and animal tracks were clearly visible in the sage-green waste. It is difficult to comprehend why that tailings mountain was just left there.

Further on was a veritable junkyard of industrial-sized vehicles that had long ago been used in this once busy mine. To our right, the buckets that had carried the payload of ore with the rich seams of asbestos down to the mill below, now hung drunkenly from the rusting tramline that snaked up the side of the mountain.

We drove on into the valley where, years before, the vibrant mining town of Cassiar had flourished. Now, what had been the town's streets were covered over with verdant undergrowth and a profusion of wild flowers, while the cooling breeze wafted tall grasses gently from side to side. The mountain ranges that I had come to know and love still towered on either side of the place, and I could recognize the hill we had skied down with such *joie de vivre*.

I tried to get my bearings as Sally and I walked around the town that was no more. I had brought an old photograph album with me and, by studying the topography carefully and turning my album this way and that, I thought I eventually located the approximate position of the hospital. But it was all guesswork. There was not a single building left. Everything had gone: the Royal Bank, the school, the dining hall, the recreation centre, even the gaol. Not a trace of foundations remained in the once bustling streets, not a single brick or piece of wood. Nothing.

My initial shock at the desolation around us was followed by a wave of sadness and nostalgia, but after a while I began to feel much better. In truth, as I started to imagine the wilderness clawing its way back, reclaiming the land that rightfully belonged to nature, I even began to feel good about the fate of Cassiar. With no sign left of the rapacious appetite for profit that had commandeered this beautiful part of British

240

Columbia, the wild animals and bird-life could return, their only disturbance a small jade mine based a few miles further down the Stuart Highway, which branches off the Alaska Highway at Watson Lake.

As we began to drive away, I saw a remnant of the curling rink, its roof partially collapsed. Only that, and the rusting vehicles, remained in this now forgotten valley, whose mountains remain one of the richest sources of asbestos in the world.

No more use for it now, this once miracle ore, impervious to water, that would not burn or decay, but had wreaked such unforeseen and tragic havoc on thousands of people all over the developed world.

Looking at that tailings pile, I remembered those who perished at Aberfan, and the kindness of the miners of Cassiar on hearing of the disaster.

We exited the valley and picked up speed. I did not look back.

*   *   *

A major disappointment of my return to Cassiar had been the failure to find any of the First Nations people, let alone make contact with them.

Later, back at Whitehorse, thanks to Susan Williams, a nurse friend of Sally's, I learned that some forty First Nations people live scattered in and around the Good Hope Lake area, members of the Johnny and Dennis family groups. Those names were familiar to me, and would be descendants of the same band who were there in the 1960s. They are members of the Tahltan community linked to Watson Lake.

241

Susan gave me the details of how to contact the office in Dease Lake that administers to the needs of the Tahltan people, but all message boxes of each of their six extensions were full and no one responded to my calls. Two of those extensions were dedicated to drug and alcohol abuse helplines.

Was this always to be the price paid by indigenous peoples whose way of life is invaded and disrespected, I wondered? Or are the First Nations people just part of the wider picture in Western society, where the damaged and disillusioned among us struggle to survive in the urban jungles by turning to drugs and alcohol for short-term relief—only to reap long-term misery?

This simple trip down memory lane, which I had hoped would reconnect me with the people and places I had known, proved insufficient to meet up with the past. That would need far more time than I had left on this visit. But the world rolls on regardless, and I had to prepare for my next port of call: Eskimo Point.

Would I fare any better there, I asked myself, or is going back never a good idea?

28

Arctic Circles

I hate deadlines. They make me feel like a bird with clipped wings, but sorry as I was to leave Whitehorse, I was on a tight schedule for my next appointment with the past: a return to Eskimo Point. Except it was no longer Eskimo Point but Arviat, 'the place of the bowhead whale'.

Getting there involved an overnight stay and a change of plane in Winnipeg, a thriving city in itself but situated in the endless expanse of Manitoba farmland which characterizes that part of Canada. As the businessman sitting next to me drily commented, 'Canada has stunning scenery, but this sure isn't it!'

The airport hotel where I'd pre-booked a room was crowded with men coming and going from the oil and gas fields of Northern Alberta's booming petroleum production industry. Roughnecks and roustabouts, electricians and drillers, welders and engineers knocked back their cold beers in the large bar, where the experienced waitresses were well able to cope with the ribald humour surrounding them. The more restrained sat in the peaceful lounge areas, their sweat-stained stetsons or dusty baseball caps pushed back from tired faces as they read newspapers, sipped cool drinks and talked quietly among themselves.

After a good—and thankfully quiet—night's sleep, I caught the early flight north on the second leg of my journey to Rankin Inlet, in the vast territory of Northern Canada, and the gateway to my destination.

The Hawker Siddeley 748, belonging to the comfortingly named Calm Air, the plane that would take me to Rankin Inlet, had a configuration I hadn't come across before. Despite its generous size and wide-bodied fuselage, there was room for only twelve passengers on this particular flight because an enormous amount of cargo was loaded into two-thirds of the aircraft. We handful of travellers were separated from the cargo by a metal partition to the front of us. This unusual arrangement only added to the undercurrent of anticipation and excitement I was feeling at the thought of being once again in the Arctic.

During the flight I got into conversation with the young Inuit woman who was sitting next to me. Margaret Igloolik was studying at teacher-training college in Winnipeg and was on her way to spend the weekend at home in Rankin, where her small daughter was living with her grandparents. Margaret told me that she had been keenly aware during her schooldays that the only Inuit staff at her high school were teaching assistants or cleaners, and she had resolved then to one day change that status quo. Margaret planned to teach English and Inuktituk once she graduated, and was determined not only to provide for her daughter, Rosie, but to encourage her to educate herself as well as possible in order to secure her future. 'You cannot always rely on the child's father,' explained Margaret.

When we disembarked at Rankin, there was Rosie in the arms of her grandmother, wriggling

244

and squealing with delight as soon as she beheld her mother. She was well named, an adorable rosy-cheeked little girl, with shining black hair gathered into two bunches and tied with pink ribbon. I gave Margaret a 'good luck with your studies, you'll be a great teacher' hug, blew a kiss to Rosie—who giggled and blew one right back—and settled down to wait for the last leg of my journey. It was a long wait: four hours. Arviat, I was told, was shrouded in thick fog—a common occurrence during the short summer months—making it impossible to fly until it had cleared somewhat.

Eventually we were able to depart, this time in an eight-seater Beechcraft copiloted by a young Inuit called Dave from Baker Lake. I watched him load my bag into the nose cone of the little plane and thought, rather incongruously, that if we crashed my bag would be the first to go for a burton!

There were two other passengers: a rugged wilderness photographer from Toronto called Mel, and a physiotherapist from Winnipeg on her routine visit to Arviat to follow up on her patients. Dave welcomed us on board, gave us the spiel about safety, and handed out fluffy white towels impregnated with an anti-bacterial agent against the currently prevalent and much feared H1N1 flu virus. Then he swivelled himself round on his haunches, slid smoothly into his copilot's seat, put on his headset and we were off.

The small plane was incredibly noisy, making any verbal communication impossible during the 45-minute flight. For this I was only too thankful since it allowed me to immerse myself in the spectacular views from the air of the mighty

Hudson Bay over which we were flying.

During my previous stay, I had only ever seen the Bay as an indistinguishable frozen expanse of white, seamlessly merging with the tundra stretching endlessly to a distant horizon. Now it lay below me in varying shades of blue, depending on the depth: violet to azure, then a periwinkle shade melting into turquoise and, finally, the delicate robin's-egg paleness of the shallows. Narrow spits of yellowy brown marked the uneven coastline. Twice Dave signalled furiously for us to look out of the left-hand windows, and there they were: pods of beluga whale! Their distinctive white bulk showed up clearly even from this great height, and I tried taking photographs. Unfortunately, the height, the speed and my excitement evidently took their toll—the quality of the pics was, to say the very least, disappointing.

Shortly after, we arrived with a bump at Arviat and rolled to a stop.

The steep metal ladder was dropped into place, and I set foot once again in the land of the Inuit, now renamed Nunavut, meaning 'Our Land'.

It had been hot and sticky in Whitehorse and Winnipeg, with temperatures in the high thirties. Now we stepped out into 15° C and a keen breeze. I pulled my all-weather Devon jacket tight and headed for the small, wooden terminal building. It was very different from my first arrival, when I had been totally shocked by the onslaught of the winter climate of minus-fifty, blinded by a howling gale, and wondering where the hell my curiosity had led me!

The bowhead whale, in whose honour Eskimo Point was renamed Arviat, has a huge head with which to break through the thick ice of Arctic waters, and with its twelve-inch-plus layer of blubber is the creature most adapted to the freezing waters. Historically, between the 1840s and early 1920s, this species was severely depleted by commercial harvesting, targeted because they were big and slow and thus relatively easy to catch. Inuit have always hunted the whales for food and fuel. Now the hunting quota is strictly regulated by the International Whaling Commission.

Dave cheerfully unloaded the bags and supplies from the plane, and then drove me over to my accommodation. The guy did everything, and whatever he was paid was surely insufficient.

From the outside, the Katimavik Suites, as my digs were known, looked like a very large metal trailer with wooden steps leading up to the front door. Inside, it was warm and cosy and spotlessly clean, with comfortable self-catering accommodation for up to a dozen guests.

After a mug of strong tea, I took a walk to see if I could get my bearings. About ten minutes' stroll along the main drag, I was attracted by the sight of some eighteen Hondas, the quad-bike-type vehicles with enormous tyres, that it seemed many families owned. They were parked randomly outside a building festooned with a Kentucky Fried Chicken sign. Inside, the place was filled with young children, teenagers and mothers with toddlers, all eating buckets of French fries and 'popcorn'—unidentifiable bits of chicken battered and deep-fried—as well as the regular chunks of fowl. A separate, and longer, line-up was made up of folks waiting to buy larger buckets to take away. So, junk food had reached the Arctic. My heart sank.

As I viewed the scene, I began ticking the imaginary boxes in my nurse's brain marked obesity, heart disease, hypertension, diabetes— closely followed by dental decay—as I watched very young children clamouring for the variously highly coloured colas and other fizzy drinks for sale.

It was the first of many walks round the settlement over the next eight days. I observed everything keenly and spoke with many residents, noting the changes from what I remembered so vividly. From what I saw and heard, together with people I met and talked to in Rankin Inlet, and in Winnipeg on my return journey, I was able to build a coherent picture of what the place had become.

My first impression was that the settlement I had known looked run-down, neglected and dreary. In all fairness, this would have been much to do with the time of year. In August there is no blanket of deep snow covering the ground, and the stark, pristine beauty that so typifies the frozen tundra was absent in the short summer months. Now, I found that the permafrosted dirt roads were little more than a succession of water-filled potholes, providing a playground for little gangs of children who splashed in the large, muddy puddles, stopping to stare solemnly at this stranger in town. *Komatiks*, those large, wooden sleds pulled by dogs, that glide easily over the frozen snow in winter, now lay abandoned, clumsy and immobile, like beached whales left high and dry by the thaw after the long, hard winter.

Dogs lay beneath most dwellings, safely chained and carefully watching as I ambled past at a safe distance. The buildings were much larger than I remembered, and mostly of a khaki, brown, or similarly dark colour, but all were still raised on strong stilts about a metre off the ground, which is what kept the dwellings stable in the permafrost. The smaller matchbox homes I remembered, painted in dolly-mixture shades of buttermilk, blue, pink and green, were all but gone; though a very few did remain, standing like sentinels echoing the past.

Most depressingly, rubbish lay strewn everywhere, even out on the tundra. Dirty nappies tossed thoughtlessly aside, plastic bottles, old tins, and all the other detritus that so blights the developed world, was now evident in this remote place. Many homes displayed piles of caribou antlers on the roof, stacked against walls and, occasionally, one nailed next to a door-frame on which to conveniently hang parkas, ropes and other heavy-duty gear.

I realised that the people in the Arctic settlements live most of their year in the snow and ice that covers up the traces of man and makes everything look clean and sparkling. But it was soon apparent that no one bothered too much about the aesthetics of their surroundings, or the possible consequences of unhygienic habits, during the short summer months. Their time and energy was spent on enjoying walks and picnics out on the tundra, picking blueberries and wild flowers and just revelling in the comparatively warm weather. Those who still hunted were out looking for food for the long winter ahead, and preparing it for storage. Meat sold for a steep $12 per pound in the store; by comparison, taking your rifle and heading out on the land could bring a 100lbs of caribou meat in one afternoon.

I watched one such hunter, George Nangiayuk, and his wife Lizzie slicing up his fresh catch of beluga whale and packing it into cardboard boxes ready to store in the nearby community freezer. George worked out how many years had passed since I had nursed in Eskimo Point—as I couldn't help still thinking of Arviat—and, as he was thirty-one years old, he decided I was probably the midwife who delivered him. I certainly remembered his mother's name—Gracie Nangiayuk. Excited at the thought, he offered me a chunky, glistening slice of *muktaq*, the raw blubber of the beluga, which was balanced on his knife—and considered a delicacy. With difficulty I managed to get some down, it would have been rude not to. Later, I sat on the end of my bed expecting my guts to rebel violently at some point, but no, nothing happened, and I actually had a good night's sleep.

George explained that the men still caught the whales with harpoons, then shot them. The haul was taken to a spit of land about two miles from the settlement, where the whales were gutted and sectioned off before being brought ashore to the settlement. The reason the entrails were left well away was because polar bears would descend to eat them, and were a danger so close to people. That was another problem that had not existed in the 1970s. Polar bears were never seen anywhere close to town. Now, two men on Hondas, rifles slung across their backs, patrolled the perimeters of Arviat on the lookout for bears, who were often seen scavenging out at the dump. With the icecap

250

melting, there are fewer and smaller icebergs where the bears can hunt for seals; as their world shrinks, and they become hungrier, they are raiding settlements in their search for food. One had read and heard about the threat to the survival of bears in the Arctic, but being actually confronted with the reality of it gives pause for thought.

I suppose I had harboured the romantic notion that the people living in what had once been an isolated part of the world would be protected from junk food, junk entertainment and junk ideas; that they would instead stick with their tried and trusted ways of living within their natural world. But as I continued my wanderings I saw the flickering reflections of television screens at most of the windows. In the two main stores, every kind of unhealthy sugary confectionery was sold. Very large plasma-screen TVs were stacked high. Graffiti blighted an assortment of buildings, emblazoning them with sentiments such as 'No bitches wanted here' or 'Fuck off'. Back in my room I had a choice between watching an array of soap operas or straight-to-video B-movies depicting gang warfare, drug abuse and crude sex and violence. Is this really the best of what our modern world has to share? Along with rolling news channels reporting violent events in Iraq or Afghanistan or Libya or Gaza or ... the list is endless.

Many teenage girls in Arviat and the region become pregnant, and have a pretty relaxed—some might say casual—attitude to adoption. If someone wants a baby, they can have one, and the girls just give it away after an arrangement made

251

on a handshake. These are known as custom adoptions and are quite common, with the result that so-called uncles, aunties and cousins are just as likely to be the parent. Some babies are adopted by people out of the settlement. A welfare payment of $200 a month is given for each child. Health issues in the community run the usual gamut of gastrointestinal upsets and chest infections (which now include superbugs like MRSA), sexually transmitted diseases, of course, and drug and alcohol abuse—all too familiar where culture clashes occur between indigenous peoples and the white interlopers from a material world. Incest and paedophilia occur, as they do in most countries and cultures wherever large families share one room—sometimes one mattress.

One can, however, be thankful that foetal alcohol syndrome is decreasing. I did see several young teenagers showing the symptoms of FAS, but education about the dangers of drinking alcohol while pregnant is now widespread, and has been for the past forty years. The indigenous women are now much more aware than they were in the 1960s and '70s. Arviat is a dry settlement, but bootlegging is a major headache for the elders and the police to control. Alcohol is brought in on boats during the summer months, and smuggled in on planes, or driven from Churchill in Bombardiers, the heavy-duty vehicles used to transport fuel drums and trucks.

I was surprised to learn that very few babies are now delivered at the health centre. Most women soon to give birth are shipped down south to Winnipeg, and it's often seen as a badge of merit to have your baby there. There are seven nurses—a mix of Canadian, Filipino, Dutch and Inuit—attached to the health centre, but none of them live there and office hours are strictly observed. The nurses take their turn to be on call for emergencies and over holidays and weekends, and have to be contacted at their homes.

I felt that the bond with the community was not nearly as close as it had been when Dorothy and I manned the centre, but times have changed over the years. In my day, the local people trusted us and the connection was close. It was unusual then to call in a medevac, but during my visit there were several medevacs in just the space of a few days to deal with teenage overdoses as well as women about to give birth, or those attending appointments down in Winnipeg—the sort of things we would have dealt with ourselves. In the 'good old days', the social issues were not as complicated as they are now and the fear of litigation just did not exist. Yes, the world had changed in thirty years, and not necessarily all for the good.

*   *   *

There are many signs of things to come in the Nunavut region that will inevitably—and in my opinion, tragically—spell the disappearance of the Inuit culture. There is, for example, strong talk of a highway being built from the south, through Arviat and beyond; the Arctic is home to rich uranium deposits, which are certain to be mined sometime in the future, particularly when access is made quicker and easier. This may bring a

253

measure of prosperity to some, but will doubtless begin the ruinous boom-and-bust culture that is so familiar to us. There is, it seems, nowhere on this earth that can keep the wider world away.

Meanwhile, as I saw and learned in Arviat, the Inuit population in the settlements face many difficulties. School is not yet mandatory in the Arctic, and no one seems to get behind the system to try to instil some discipline. Teachers say it is difficult to inspire young people when their parents lack motivation.

Many children come to school hungry, with only chocolate bars, sweets and cola stuffed into their pockets for lunch. The visiting dentist is often forced to extract baby teeth because they are in a state of severe decay, and more than 30 per cent of the youngsters have no teeth. For this reason, many schools have started breakfast clubs, and after-school sports activities. Distressingly, young mothers often ask for toast or a sandwich for themselves because they too are hungry. In larger communities like Rankin Inlet there are good support services for these young mothers, but not so for the smaller, more isolated settlements.

It's not universally hopeless, of course. Naturally, there *are* some students who are diligent and do succeed. Unsurprisingly, they are invariably from families with a strong work ethic, who have done well, moved along with the times, and taught their children by example.

I asked my hunter friend George about the migratory patterns of the caribou. When I left in 1979, the elders were worried that the Alaskan pipeline would disturb the wildlife that the Inuit depended so heavily upon. He laughed, and said,

'They are still talking about it, only now it is the fear of a road being built for uranium mining to open things up. We always have to worry about something.'

But disaster is not always inevitable. The Alaskan pipeline is there, the caribou are still there. They are sensitive to disturbances, and at times calving is down, but they bounce back. I spoke with a well-known wilderness guide of many years, known affectionately as 'Tundra Tom', who was passing through Arviat while I was there. A second-generation guide, taught by his father Hank, Tom Faess was raised in Northern Ontario. He leads small groups of naturalists, photographers and anyone wishing to see wolves, musk ox, caribou and moose in their natural habitat in what he calls 'the last frontier'. I asked Tom about the proposed road. He agreed that if it does happen, for sure it will deal a death blow to the traditional way of life for both Inuit and the wild animals, who have lived together in natural balance for so many generations.

I also asked about climate change. The general consensus among the elders of the community and those with years of wilderness experience, is that weather patterns are always changing, and have always been changeable, but the cyclical patterns are speeding up. All agreed the waters of the Hudson Bay had risen higher, and fishing shacks based on the shoreline for years have had to be moved a few yards to higher land. As already remarked, polar bears are hungrier and are now a danger to the settlement, and bird-life has increased over the past few years, in both numbers and varieties, as the climate has warmed and

255

seasonal behaviour has shifted.

The sad fact is that, if you are going to let the world in, you have to keep up with the world.

This was demonstrated to me when I spent a day with the industrious and jovial women at the Sewing Centre. I watched them, skilled seamstresses all, cutting patterns from sealskin for designers who visited regularly from Montreal and New York with pictures of high-fashion coats, hats, boots, mittens and parkas for the fashionistas down south. It seemed a bit incongruous, watching the women cutting intricate patterns into the sealskin and measuring them against tailors' dummies standing in the corner, but needs must, and these women were moving with the times. The once nomadic Inuit had to survive on seasonal harvests, and the seal hunt has always been a cornerstone in the fabric of Inuit social, cultural and economic life.

The skills of hunting and butchering the seals, treating the skins and selling sealskin is learned at an early age. Income earned from the sale of surplus sealskin and skin products is used to finance hunting equipment and supplies. This continues to put food on the table in this land of scant vegetation and prohibitive costs for imported foods. The seamstresses used to call the seal 'truly our daily bread'.

While I was there, the women were also busy making little sealskin lapel loops for everyone to wear as a protest against the ban on seal hunting. Theirs is not a frivolous pastime. Seal hunting, historically, has always meant survival, and is still an important part of the Inuit people's food chain.

The Arctic remains one of the last frontiers—

for the time being. But it is easy to see that things are changing. It will take another couple of generations before the young people of the Arctic gain a steadier foothold on life. They are beginning to confront exactly the same issues that blight our own societies in the more developed world.

I still fail to understand why every generation has to repeat the same mistakes as the last, that we seem unable to learn from each other. What I *do* understand is that watching vacuous soap operas and violent films, and living off fast food, drugs and alcohol is not the way forward. And, sadly, I'm not too sure that high fashion, optimistically and skilfully stitched by these wonderful ladies, can hold back time either.

*   *   *

All too soon it was time to leave. I felt dissatisfied, needful of so much more time to try and understand what I had seen and heard in the Arctic. Of course I did understand that, like many other places in the world, change is unavoidable, but I suppose in an isolated place such as this, the changes seem so much more stark. I remember watching some *mutawah* (religious men) in Saudi Arabia shooting at satellite dishes that began appearing on roofs, and how shocked they were to see US Army women driving military buses and trucks during the first Gulf War. We were witnessing a terrific clash of cultures, and that is what I was seeing here. It will take a few generations for people to find their comfort level in this changing world.

Unless I can return one hundred years from now, I do not wish to go back. A period of great change and turbulence lies ahead, and only the young people can build their future. Meanwhile, I felt—and feel—privileged to have experienced something of the world these Inuit people inhabit, and to have known many amazing members of their community.

What, I wondered somewhat apprehensively, would I find had happened to the Australian Aborigines in and around Alice Springs, where I was planning to return in a few weeks' time?

29

Outside Looking In

In mid-November 2009, thirty-five years after I had left Alice Springs behind, I set off on another long-haul journey to see how the place and its people had fared since. The southern hemisphere summer is not the most sensible time to spend eighteen days in the Red Centre of Australia—too damned hot. And so it was in 2009, but time and money were not on my side, and, anyway, I've never been known for my perfect timing.

From Canada, it was back to London in order to travel halfway round the world in the other direction. The flights to Alice Springs, via Heathrow, Singapore and Perth, were comfortable, efficient and on time, but it all took a good twenty-four hours, during which time I ate two breakfasts, one dinner and something that was meant to be lunch, not to mention some indeterminate in-between snacks. I also watched two forgettable movies, and I *did* sleep: for a whole ten minutes with my head slumped on a coffee cup on my tray, which left an attractive indentation across my forehead and cheek. I adjusted my watch three times en route, and learned that we had gained eleven hours. My inner clock was wrecked by the time we touched down in temperatures of 44° C at what, according to Alice Springs, was 4 p.m. the following day!

Once in the terminal building, drenched with sweat and my make-up sliding down my face, I was met by Ted, the hotel driver. We chatted amiably as we trundled through the red-brick dustbowl and sparse scrubland into town. He told me he had lived in Alice since the 1960s, and was amazed I had bothered with a return visit.

'You'll find the town pretty much the same,' he told me, 'but attitudes have hardened. It's not as friendly as it used to be. Everything goes to the black fellas; the government gives them too much sittin' down money and they spend it at the casino. Cab drivers are all bloody drongos from someplace else, but while the beer stays cold I reckon Alice is as good a place as any,' was Ted's cheerful comment.

After checking in at the hotel, I made straight for the small bar and ordered a Victoria Bitter— my first cold Aussie beer in many a long year. For a split second I wondered if anyone would mind terribly if I just poured it over my sweaty head, but instead I drank the reviving amber nectar, relishing the delicious cool sensation as it slid down my dry throat.

Up in my comfortable room I checked the

259

spacious bathroom, looked out the window at an expanse of red dirt, flicked on the TV and ate half the complimentary box of chocolates—like you do when you're semi-comatose with exhaustion and excitement! Then I showered, sat on the bed, felt sick from the chocolate overload, and watched TV in some confusion: there, on the small screen, was *Songs of Praise*, beaming in from Truro Cathedral in Cornwall, just down the road from where my sister Joan lived!

International travel is really weird these days, I thought again, and then I slept for fourteen hours straight.

* * *

The hotel, and the town generally, were pretty empty of tourists. Wrong time of year, and way too hot. The best time to visit Alice is in April when there is more greenery, and the heat is subsiding, and just before the crowds begin arriving between May and September. But a few hardy souls were braving it. Backpackers sat out the heat in internet cafés and beer parlours, and I spotted a few more experienced Aussie tourists, determined in their four-wheel-drive camper vans as they stocked up with huge amounts of water for the next long leg of their outback adventure. This kind of heat is dangerous, and no place for first-timers trekking across the vast tracts of desert. Grizzled truck drivers occasionally dropped in for a night or two while their vehicles were emptied, loaded, serviced, or swapped over with others. And the occasional artist or writer, travelling around and looking for inspiration, would turn up, hoping to find it in a hotel bar in Alice.

Despite the obvious passage of time, and the cosmetic differences one would expect, I was immediately reminded of the special feel that this vibrant outback town has. Balanced awkwardly between deserts, surrounded by parched bushland and at the mercy of extreme temperatures, it is the dramatic beauty of this landscape that one never forgets. The burning sun as it rises and sets throws a plethora of colours across rock pools, sacred sites and mountains. From the brick-red of sunrise, to the soft indigo of evening, the light is exquisite in this central area.

It is home to prehistoric-looking lizards, venomous snakes and exotic bird-life and, despite months of searing heat, a fleeting shower of rain can bring the desert alive for a day with glorious carpets of defiant little yellow and white flowers. As the rain disappears, so do the blooms, as if they were but a mirage. The next rains might be many months away, but those flowers wait patiently, somehow surviving the harsh conditions before breaking out in their finery once more.

I was reminded of the same pattern of flora that suddenly appears on the tundra at the first sign of the fleeting Arctic summer; carpets of dainty mauve blossoms turning the recently frozen waste into a natural garden, before withdrawing when the onslaught of the long winter begins.

*   *   *

I was again surrounded by the straight-talking, blunt honesty of these people, and I loved it.

When nursing in Vietnam, the American

soldiers due for an R & R (rest and recreation) trip had several choices of destination to choose from. Hawaii was first choice for the married men. Hong Kong, Penang and Bangkok were also popular. But the place all the single men raved about was Sydney, Australia. And not just for the obvious pleasures. They spoke highly and affectionately of the direct Aussie sense of humour, their love of sport and their fierce loyalty to the flag of their country.

The next two weeks unfolded like a colourful patchwork quilt of memories, some happy, others less so.

I recalled the laughter, the tears, and the dark secrets of my long-ago sojourn. Those 'dark secrets' hit me much more forcibly now: as a more mature, more thoughtful person, more experienced in the often cruel ways of the world, I found myself wondering how in the past I was unaware of the injustices of racism which were so obvious to me on this trip.

I walked around town trying to get my bearings as I had done at Arviat, but in a place that couldn't be more different. Anzac Hill, with its panoramic views towards the foothills of the McDonnell ranges just over a mile to the south, soon sorted me out. Now with a population of 27,000, the town of Alice Springs had almost doubled in size from the 14,000 people to whom it was home in the early 1970s. Many of the buildings of character had gone, replaced with newer, sleeker hotels and restaurants, some serving excellent cuisine and at reasonable prices. I found a place serving barramundi. That fish has to be the best in the world and was a firm favourite of Matt and myself.

The Todd Mall, with racks of brightly coloured cotton clothes displayed on the sidewalks, had always been the focal point for visitors to this outback town. Now, despite this being low season, the craft shops and the little cafés, ranging from bistros to sizzling Asian stir-fry joints, were ticking over.

Aboriginal art in all its forms—from magnificent works hung tastefully in expensive galleries, to decorated keyring tabs, stubby holders and bottle openers in little stores overflowing with tat—was everywhere to be seen. The distinctive work of the many gifted local painters is easy to recognize, yet the only Aboriginal people I saw in and around the mall—and the town generally— were dejected little groups sitting in little circles on the grass of the small park areas, just watching the world go by. The world gave barely a glance in return. Some of these people had rolled-up paintings tucked away at their side, or in a cloth bag. It took me a few days to realize this.

One day I came upon an elderly couple sitting in the shade. The old man was painting on a piece of canvas, placing white and ochre dots in a thoughtful pattern. He worked slowly and deliberately, his eyes never straying from his task. His snow-white hair was partially hidden by his large, battered bush hat, which sported a green feather, a ballpoint pen and a razor blade tucked into the band. Next to the canvas lay an old wooden box containing little pots of blue, black, yellow and red paint.

The lady at his side, wearing a baggy floral dress and a frayed cardigan buttoned haphazardly, smiled shyly when I said hello, reminding me of those I used to visit in the riverbed camps thirty-five years before. I recognised the stillness of the desert in the old lady's eyes and felt a tug at my heartstrings as I noticed the resignation in the slump of her shoulders—resignation that suggested her acceptance of the fact that she was invisible to the folk hurrying along the mall. Nobody was going to pay her much heed and she knew it. I recognized the familiar smell of lives lived around campfires; smoke mixed with the musk of bodies unwashed due to scarcity of water. You never forget the smell of poverty. I felt sad that, in their eyes, I was just another overweight, white tourist; I could no longer be the friendly nurse, able to reach so much more closely into their lives as I had been in the past. Perhaps, I thought, as I looked at this couple, I was making mistaken assumptions about them, as surely they were about me.

A lot of that goes on in life.

Nearby, a larger group of younger indigenous people sat, some with children. The little ones sucked on the bones of Kentucky Fried Chicken, the wrappers from which lay strewn about them. From this lot came cursing, raised voices, and a bubbling undertone of resentment and irritability as they watched people walking by. Young policemen in their smart beige tropical uniforms stood in the shade nearby, seemingly staring into space, but actually watching their every move, and missing nothing.

It was here that I became confused at the unmissable sight and sound of a large group of giggling teenage girls. Every single one of them had bite marks alongside two bloody puncture

264

wounds on their exposed, white necks. At first I thought the heat must be playing tricks with my mind. But it turned out they were rushing to buy tickets for the Alice Springs premiere of the second blockbuster film in the *Twilight* saga—*New Moon*. These scars were the mark of a prized kiss from the hunky, bloodsucking vampire Edward Cullen. I looked at the indigenous people sitting on the grass of the Todd Mall, and looked at the girls. The words 'primitive behaviour' nibbled at the corner of my mind as I strolled past the beauticians' shop doing a roaring trade in fake vampire kisses. Progress, you can't beat it.

Over a few days I looked out for the older couple, carefully choosing my moment to ask about the painting.

'You give me fifty dollars then I tell you the story,' the old man said, without looking up. The old lady smiled apologetically. I pointed out the river, the snake and the moon in his painting of dots and lines.

'How do you know this?' he asked.

I told them how I had been in Alice before, and what I had learned in my few years there. How much I like Albert Namatjira watercolours and have a print of one at home in England.

The old man looked up at me, squinting into the sun, and said, 'For fifty dollars, you can have this. For a picture of my country, I will take fifty dollars from you, but it is not yet finished. Come back tomorrow if you want it.'

With a cheery goodbye, I strolled away and went for a cool drink at a nearby café, whose owner warned me not to buy anything from 'those bloody thieves. Their paintings are no bloody good, they're just beggars and you are encouraging them. The police are always moving them on because they're a bloody nuisance round these parts. And don't give them money. It takes business away from the shopkeepers.'

Next day I returned to buy the painting, but the old couple were not there.

*   *   *

Yirara College is a complex of sprawling buildings that lie in the sparse shade of white gum trees, some three miles out of town on the airport road. It had opened with great excitement and optimism in the mid-1970s, shortly before I left Alice Springs. Mistakes were made, as you would expect. Aboriginal children, suddenly finding themselves housed in dormitories, hated having a solid roof over their heads and would sneak out to sleep under the stars. This led to bulldozers being brought in to create artificial dry-riverbeds, billabongs or *wadis*, in order to make the children feel closer to their roots. It seemed a shambles at the time, but at least clumsy attempts were being made to bridge the colliding worlds.

I was both curious and keen to see how the college had developed and arranged to visit there one morning. Unfortunately, I arrived to find a power cut was causing much consternation. Computers lay idle, and lack of air conditioning and fans left the staff, not to mention me, sticky in the oppressive, late-November air. Nonetheless, great improvements had been made since I last saw the school, and particularly since 1993, when the school had been taken over by the Lutheran

Church of Australia at the request of parents who wanted the establishment to have a more Christian focus. The pastor and several of the chaplains attached to the school are now indigenous Aboriginals; at the time of my visit the pastor was in New York, attending an international conference about ways forward for the education and integration of indigenous students.

Parents see this residential and co-educational school as a place of safety for their children, under the watchful eye of people they trust and out of the way of the alcohol and drugs so freely available in town. The children, aged from twelve to sixteen, are taught with a strong emphasis on life skills, learning to understand the importance of citizenship alongside their vocational and academic development. Sport plays an essential part with swimming, 'footie' (Australian rules football), basketball and netball pursued enthusiastically and in competition with other schools in the Territory—and, indeed, throughout Australia. At age fifteen, students have the opportunity to participate in on-campus work placements, which gives them valuable work experience in preparation for the world outside.

Glass cases line the walls of the college building displaying the smiling faces of boys and girls proudly showing off their achievements in metalwork, carpentry, fashion design and art. Photographs of football, netball and baseball teams abound, showing the students, plus their medals and trophies, standing to attention in straight lines several rows deep, and smiling proudly into the camera.

However, heart-warming and encouraging as

this all was, and is, the take-up of actual jobs in town is disappointingly low. Gail, the headteacher, who had previously taught in Canada and China as well as Adelaide, had been in post for only six months, but her calm optimism was infectious. Gail explained that family ties are very strong among Aboriginals. Once returned to their communities, or settlements, many sink back into the local scene and choose to live in their own bubble. A few are employed for their carpentry and metalwork skills, repairing furniture, or homes that have been trashed, or that just need a facelift. Role models are invited to visit the school, but most children look on politely, with few interested in a future that might take them away from their communities. Even the thought of travelling to South Australia to study and further themselves is apparently unappealing to most of the students.

As I looked into the open, eager faces in the photographs, I felt thankful that I am a 'glass half full' kind of person. I continue to hope that the optimism and naivety of these young indigenous Australians won't lead them into swift disillusionment when they leave college for the outside world. The take-up rate for careers like teaching, nursing or medicine is slow, but it *is* happening and will increase in time.

Another problem for these young people is that the need for stockmen, and those displaying horsemanship skills generally, still required in some areas in the north and south of Australia, is now dying out in the Northern Territory and the Darwin area. Gail told me that some of the children speak of their grandfathers and fathers having been stockmen. But now helicopters are used to round up the brumbies. Standing in that school I realized that, much as we think things are changing rapidly, truly effective, positive and long-lasting change needs time. A lot of time.

*   *   *

Things *are*, however, moving forward, albeit slowly. In 1914, an Aboriginal woman named Topsy Smith was the first destitute indigenous person to turn up in Alice Springs. She was seeking shelter with her seven half-caste children following the death of her partner, a white man who was a miner working the gold mines in Arltunga, who was their much-loved father. The local authority built her a basic shed in which to live and soon, as she was followed to Alice by an ever-increasing community of babies and children, teenagers, orphans and abandoned mothers, many more sheds were built, but conditions were primitive, indeed, abysmal. The Federal Government colluded with the Church in the belief that children of part Aboriginal descent were a threat to the fabric of white society.

Nonetheless, in 1932, the children were moved to what became known as The Bungalow, outside of the town, in the charge of a matron, but conditions remained grim and physical and mental abuse were rife. The children were damaged by the constant message that the Aborigine in them was a cause for shame, and they were encouraged to eradicate their cultural roots and forget their language. I was immediately reminded of Connie, the Cree Indian woman in Whitehorse I had met just a few months earlier. The same policies wreaked the same havoc among the indigenous people on both continents. The mixed-race children were forbidden to speak their own language, as the road to civilisation was seen to be attainable only through the formal education of the white man's world.

The Bungalow closed in 1960 but Charles Perkins, one of the many young children raised there, went on to become a great Australian with an outstanding political career. In the mid-'70s, Charlie was an outspoken political activist and very much a part of the local political scene in Alice Springs. I met him on a couple of occasions when he called in at the hospital to visit the patients, or dropped into the riverbed camps. He fought ceaselessly against injustices perpetrated by whites against his people, taking part in the Freedom Rides across Australia in the mid-'60s which echoed the Civil Rights movement in the USA; he was also a professional football player and, as a graduate of the University of Sydney, the first Aborigine to obtain a university degree.

Today Topsy Smith is widely respected and honoured in the National Pioneer Women's Hall of Fame and her great-granddaughter Linda Smith Penangke has created a famous painting of her called *Arltunga to Alice Springs*. In Alice Springs, where she encountered such degrading treatment in 1914, there is now a decent refuge called the Topsy Smith Hostel.

Yes, things have certainly got better ...

* * *

I wanted to walk along the dry Todd riverbed to

see if I could find any of the camps I remembered well so, in an attempt to beat the heat, I rose early one morning to explore.

Once there, I found the white sand strewn with bone-dry twigs and leaves that crackled beneath my feet. The ghostly white gum trees with their peeling trunks were no protection against the golden globe of sun that rose swiftly and began to burn through my cotton shirt. I had a large bottle of water, which I tried to eke out as I walked along. Apart from some discarded bottles and beer cans lying on the ground, there was little evidence that any people were around—that is, until a couple of policemen arrived on the scene. They asked me who I was and where I was going, and when I explained they—being too polite to laugh- escorted me back to the road nearby and told me never to walk there again.

'Way too dangerous for you to be alone down here,' they said. 'Things are not as you remember them.' They drove me back to my hotel, and that was that.

Clearly, retracing my steps was not going to be easy.

I used taxis quite a bit, as it was way too hot to walk everywhere and too expensive to hire a car. I was surprised at the array of nationalities among cab drivers. There were several Indian Sikhs among them, a Sri Lankan and an Italian; I met people from the Lebanon and Syria, from Egypt and Romania, and found a number of Sudanese and Ugandan drivers.

Alice Springs, I realised, had become a microcosm of what was happening in communities over much of the Western world. The mix of cultures living and working there was very different from how I remembered the town. Surely, I thought, this was progress, a good thing? But prejudice and resentment was voiced all too readily and clearly by many people I spoke with.

Returning to my hotel one evening, the reception staff encouraged me to watch a movie called *Samson and Delilah* that was being shown that night on Channel 8. I had never heard of it, but local interest was intense. This was not surprising since, as well as having won the Caméra d'Or for a first film at the Cannes Festival, it was written and directed by Warwick Thornton, himself part indigenous Australian.

I sat riveted, and I urge anyone who rents DVDs to watch this extraordinary film depicting life in today's communities in the Alice Springs area. It calls attention to the tragedy and exploitation of the largely ignored rural Aboriginal community. The dead-end stillness of life on a settlement is captured with painful accuracy for white viewers.

Uncomfortable certainly, and deeply moving, it follows the love between a couple of teenagers who look out for each other. It catches exactly the boredom and emptiness of life for those who do not quite fit in their own country. I was astounded at the quality of acting. The cast was mainly chosen from among residents of Alice and the vicinity, and were not professional actors. Maybe that is what makes the film so real. These people were not acting: they were just living out their normal, everyday lives for the camera.

Samson and Delilah made me squirm in discomfort, even as I applauded the honesty and courage of Warwick Thornton and his brave cast.

*　　　*　　　*

At last I visited the hospital that had been at the centre of my life in Alice Springs, and found that the building I knew so well had long gone to be replaced by a faceless and functional modern building. Knots of Aborigines hung around, sitting under the trees across the road from the main entrance, some with bandaged heads, or legs, or arms. Children with snotty noses grumbled in the heat, babies nuzzled at their mothers' breasts. All of these people waiting, just like they did in the '70s ... For what? Outpatient appointments? A relative to be discharged? A better life to come along? Or maybe hoping the Dreamtime would give them a signal that the good old days would return.

I spent a few hours at the hospital, but it seemed to have lost something in the intervening years. It was just another modern healthcare facility that looked like dozens of others. The emergency room was cramped and bustling with the usual mixture of those injured, sick or inebriated. Nurses and doctors looked focused and efficient as they went about their duties.

I was surprised to find the children's ward was almost empty. The head nurse was kind and friendly and took valuable time to answer my questions. In this heat, I had expected to find the ward busy with toddlers suffering from various gastro problems, but medical care out on the settlements has improved greatly over the years. Comprehensive health care programmes have been initiated in communities with the Aboriginal

273

Congress body committed to 'keeping Aboriginal health in Aboriginal hands'.

Large investment has enabled the development of new programmes to tackle health problems out on the settlements. The names of some of these initiatives reflect typical Aussie straight-talking: the busy alcohol treatment and rehabilitation programme and team is officially called The Grog Mob and a primary-care service for young people focusing on mental health issues is called Headspace.

There were various other facilities around town which purported to work 'with' or 'for' the indigenous people. I visited these too, invariably coming away with glossy brochures that had been pressed into my hands. These were crammed with statistics: alcohol-related abuse decreased by fourteen per cent in town; stabbings reduced from two hundred per annum to seventy and so on.

One can only hope that in time all these statistics will translate into real opportunities for the folk sitting on the grass in town. They are the poorest of the poor in a land of plenty—a land that always claimed to 'give everyone a fair shake'.

But there are strong role models for those shiny-faced young students at Yirara College to get excited about. There are individuals in every country whose story has the ability to make us stop in respectful amazement. For a brief, shining moment they can unite us in the knowledge that we all share a common humanity.

Such a person is Geoffrey Gurrumul Yunupingu—born blind and into poverty, this Aboriginal singer can move to tears anyone who hears the sublime quality of his voice. He has won many awards, and can count Elton John, Sting and Björk as firm fans. Geoffrey sees his role as simply telling the stories of his people and his culture. He has no need for money.

Such a story is that of Emmanuel Kelly and his brother Ahmed. Abandoned in Iraq, the little brothers were found in a box by some nuns. Both were born without limbs due to the effects *in utero* of chemical warfare. Adopted by Moira Kelly, an extraordinary Australian woman, the boys have thrived, been fitted with prosthetic limbs and are forging wonderful lives, despite their terrible start. Nineteen-year-old Ahmed is now a Paralympic swimmer, and Emmanuel recently sang in *The X Factor* in Australia. His song of choice was 'Imagine', and brought all who heard his sweet voice to their feet. His face shone as he sang of his hope that 'the world will be as one'.

Moving though the words of John Lennon are, I wonder if the world being as one is really the answer. We need a world that accepts cultural and individual differences, with equal opportunities for all, rather than a big melting pot full of nondescript sameness. So how can our modern-day world, moving at breakneck speed thanks to technology, innovation and richness of thought, be made compatible with the ancient traditions that cherish a slower, more meditative lifestyle in harmony with nature? There has to be a way of promoting and conserving both ways, and there is the rub.

*   *   *

Coming to the end of my time in Alice, I felt a bit

275

sad, as well as having nothing but respect for the spirit of those who settled this area, and certainly for those who continue to make a better life for their children in this fascinating frontier town. No matter what had changed for the better for the indigenous people, many have, down through the ages, been left on the margins: ever so politely—but ever so effectively—simply not included in the white man's society.

Yet that white man's society wrought pain and suffering on the thousands of their own little children who endured forced immigration from post-war Britain in the 1950s and '60s. I sat in my hotel room and watched Australia's then Prime Minister, Kevin Rudd, apologize to a roomful of white-haired pensioners in a hall in Canberra. Many were openly weeping, and I joined them, horrified by the realization that my own country had sent thousands of children to Australia on a false promise of fresh oranges plucked from trees and never-ending sunshine. Many had been told they were orphans, but were in fact the children of impoverished families or unmarried mothers. Bewildered, and with no one to fight their corner, separated on the dockside from brothers and sisters, some of them ended up loveless and alone in state-run orphanages or religious institutions, where they were abused emotionally and sexually.

Had Alice changed? Had I changed? Was I so naive back then? Perhaps we all go about not seeing what is really going on around us, whatever age we think we are living in.

I left Alice on my budget ticket, and began the 24-hour marathon journey in reverse, back to Heathrow via Perth and Singapore.

As I settled in my seat, I thought of my father's words many years ago, when I invited him to Alice Springs for a holiday at my expense. He gave it some thought, before declining the offer in a letter that I've kept:

Anne. Thank you. But I am going to say no. I have no interest in sitting inside a metal tube that hurtles through space, taking a bunch of people within just a few hours, to the other side of the world. I travelled to Australia many times in the Thirties and Forties.

In those days it took eight weeks, calling in at many different ports along the way, off-loading and taking on various cargos. One had a sense that one was travelling halfway around the world. You saw people's skin colour slowly change as it adapted to the climate; heard languages, observed costumes and cultures changing; felt the winds and the very air you breathed changing as we moved around the sun and the moon. Flora and fauna amazed us with their variety, and the swell of the oceans told you things were different.

Why then would I want to hurtle through space with a bunch of strangers who cannot possibly appreciate just how privileged they are to experience such extensive, life-changing travel? But thank you. I love you for the thought . . .

When he died in 1985, at the age of eighty-four, he had never experienced flight, yet had travelled many times around the globe. I envied my father this, and have often wished I had lived his experiences of discovery. That said, I believe I have followed in his wake in my own way, forging my own adventures and, most important of all, have found the magic that somehow survives in this world of ours.

Though we never discussed it, I'm sure he must have learned from his Rambling Rose that nurses do a little more than wipe other people's arses.

*   *   *

As I bring my second book to an end, my thoughts now turn back to the long and eventful journey of my life.

The shifting sands of time are something we all have to deal with, in one way or another. My life has been and still is a fascinating series of lessons in life and how to live it.

I have learned that there is nothing to be scared of out there. Treat everyone as you wish to be treated, and the universe will open up to you.

My parents, the nurse and the sailor, taught me that, and I am grateful to them both.